CCCC STUDIES IN WRITING & RHETORIC
Edited by Steve Parks, University of Virginia

The aim of the CCCC Studies in Writing & Rhetoric (SWR) Series is to influence how we think about language in action and especially how writing gets taught at the college level. The methods of studies vary from the critical to historical to linguistic to ethnographic, and their authors draw on work in various fields that inform composition—including rhetoric, communication, education, discourse analysis, psychology, cultural studies, and literature. Their focuses are similarly diverse—ranging from individual writers and teachers, to work on classrooms and communities and curricula, to analyses of the social, political, and material contexts of writing and its teaching.

SWR was one of the first scholarly book series to focus on the teaching of writing. It was established in 1980 by the Conference on College Composition and Communication (CCCC) in order to promote research in the emerging field of writing studies. As our field has grown, the research sponsored by SWR has continued to articulate the commitment of CCCC to supporting the work of writing teachers as reflective practitioners and intellectuals.

We are eager to identify influential work in writing and rhetoric as it emerges. We thus ask authors to send us project proposals that clearly situate their work in the field and show how they aim to redirect our ongoing conversations about writing and its teaching. Proposals should include an overview of the project, a brief annotated table of contents, and a sample chapter. They should not exceed 10,000 words.

To submit a proposal, please register as an author at www.editorial manager.com/nctebp. Once registered, follow the steps to submit a proposal (be sure to choose SWR Book Proposal from the drop-down list of article submission types).

Salt of the Earth

Rhetoric, Preservation, and White Supremacy

James Chase Sanchez
Middlebury College

Conference on College
Composition and
Communication

National Council of
Teachers of English

National Council of Teachers of English
340 N. Neil St., Suite #104, Champaign, Illinois 61820
www.ncte.org

Staff Editor: Bonny Graham
Manuscript Editor: Leigh Scarcliff
Series Editor: Steve Parks
Interior Design: Mary Rohrer
Cover Design: Pat Mayer
Cover Photo: James Chase Sanchez

NCTE Stock Number: 42233; eStock Number: 42240
ISBN 978-0-8141-4223-3; eISBN 978-0-8141-4224-0

It is the policy of NCTE in its journals and other publications to provide a forum for the open discussion of ideas concerning the content and the teaching of English and the language arts. Publicity accorded to any particular point of view does not imply endorsement by the Executive Committee, the Board of Directors, or the membership at large, except in announcements of policy, where such endorsement is clearly specified.

NCTE provides equal employment opportunity (EEO) to all staff members and applicants for employment without regard to race, color, religion, sex, national origin, age, physical, mental or perceived handicap/disability, sexual orientation including gender identity or expression, ancestry, genetic information, marital status, military status, unfavorable discharge from military service, pregnancy, citizenship status, personal appearance, matriculation or political affiliation, or any other protected status under applicable federal, state, and local laws.

Every effort has been made to provide current URLs and email addresses, but because of the rapidly changing nature of the web, some sites and addresses may no longer be accessible.

Library of Congress Cataloging-in-Publication Data

Names: Sanchez, James Chase, author.
Title: Salt of the earth : rhetoric, preservation, and white supremacy / James Chase Sanchez, Middlebury College.
Description: Champaign, Illinois : Conference on College Composition and Communication of the National Council of Teachers of English, [2021] | Series: Studies in Writing & Rhetoric | Includes bibliographical references and index. | Summary: "This autoethnography and cultural rhetorics case study investigates the rhetoric of white supremacy by exploring three unique rhetorical processes—identity construction, storytelling, and silencing—as they relate to an umbrella act: the rhetoric of preservation"—Provided by publisher.
Identifiers: LCCN 2021014580 (print) | LCCN 2021014581 (ebook) | ISBN 9780814142233 (Trade Paperback) | ISBN 9780814142240 (Adobe PDF)
Subjects: LCSH: Grand Saline (Tex.)—Race relations. | White supremacy movements—Texas—Grand Saline. | Rhetoric—Social aspects. | Narrative inquiry (Research method)
Classification: LCC F394.G736 S26 2021 (print) | LCC F394.G736 (ebook) | DDC 305.8009764/276--dc23
LC record available at https://lccn.loc.gov/2021014580
LC ebook record available at https://lccn.loc.gov/2021014581

This book is dedicated to Charles Moore. Though we never met, our stories are intertwined. May you rest in peace.

Also, to my grandfather, David Smith: My entire life I have always strived to make you proud. This book is a reflection of your love.

CONTENTS

FOREWORD

MY RELATIONSHIP WITH MY Grand Saline roots is nothing if not complicated.

Being a small-town girl is an important part of my identity. I was raised to value simplicity over superficiality, personal relationships over possessions, and faith over fear.

Many of the values I developed growing up in Grand Saline have continued to serve me throughout my life. Although I chose to leave my hometown at the first opportunity and occasionally wandered away from those original ideas, I've always come back to the foundation it provided me. And I take pride in that. As an adult, I've lived in larger cities—being exposed to levels of financial privilege I'd only previously seen on TV. It was the kind of flash and frivolity I'd been warned about growing up in Grand Saline. I can't say I always rose above and remembered what was important; however, I'd eventually return to what I knew to be real and lasting—family, friendship, love, compassion, and kindness. Being a nice girl who returns her cart after grocery shopping, holds the door for strangers, and always says "please" and "thank you" is who I am. It's who I am because of how I was raised, because of Grand Saline, in so many ways. For that, I'm grateful.

Unfortunately, articulating my relationship with Grand Saline doesn't end with good, honest small-town values. As an adult I've come to realize that the ways in which I felt held and cared for by my hometown were very much conditional. I won't go so far as to say that the folks in my hometown *only* loved me because I was a white evangelical in good standing; however, I believe that if I hadn't been both of those things, my experience would've been quite different. I now know and understand that I was loved not exclusively for who I was, but also because I was really great at following the rules and doing what was expected of me.

It's easy to say that Grand Saline and other towns like it have a racism problem without further explanation. And that's probably not unfair. I won't dance around the fact that the racism that continues to exist in Grand Saline is indefensible. End of story. However, I do believe understanding its roots is important when we consider how we can reach a resolution. Something I always come back to (and is likely recognizable in this book and in the documentary *Man on Fire*) is the lack of awareness that permeates the community. It's easy, it's convenient, it requires no uncomfortable introspection.

Small-town culture often involves sweeping unsightly dust under the rug, rather than acknowledging its presence and taking the necessary steps to remove it. Not looking at it and denying its existence is a defense mechanism a lot of us developed, believing denial was resilience. Examining mistakes and what led us to make them wasn't our practice. We left the past in the past and preferred never to speak of it again.

In the 1990s, Grand Saline's racism was so notable that it was reported on CBS, in a news program called *Eye on America* with Connie Chung. We'd quite literally become infamous for having no Black people in our town. I remember the days leading up to the news crew's arrival. It didn't seem that much credence was being given to the story Chung and her team were telling. In fact, it was kind of a joke—elitist rich people making judgments without merit. The overeducated coming to town with the sole purpose of criticizing our culture and way of life. I think I was ten or eleven at the time and I recall being quite confused. Wasn't Connie Chung a reputable and respected reporter? How could CBS be so far off the mark? And if they were in fact telling lies about my community, what was the payoff? What could they possibly gain in spreading falsehoods about a town so small it only had one stoplight?

This confusion only served to point to the bigger picture of my Grand Saline experience—the discrepancies between the version of Grand Saline I'd been socialized to see and the version of Grand Saline I was learning the outside world was seeing. Looking back, I realize that my own community couldn't muster up the wherewithal to accept that we might have some work to do. It was much easier to discredit the source. If we continued to deny the problem, we wouldn't have to do the work of fixing it.

I'd love to say that I was born with empathy and compassion for othered folks (be it people of color, the LGBTQIA community, or even atheists), but my understanding of privilege and white supremacy didn't come until later. By 1980s and 1990s East Texas standards, I did grow up in a somewhat progressive home (working mother who greatly contributed to the household financially, liberal-leaning father who was affectionate and nurturing), which was helpful on my journey to a deeper understanding of structural racism. Although I attended a conservative Baptist university, I had many wonderful professors who challenged the evangelical traditions and practices I'd been raised with in Grand Saline. Dr. Allen Redmon, for instance, immediately comes to mind as he was the first person who taught me about feminism, which continues to be such an important part of my perspective and identity today. I remember him teaching us that feminism wasn't exclusively about women's rights but the rights of all marginalized people. This resonated with me in a profound way and was, I believe, a meaningful step in opening my eyes to a world outside my own monolithic bubble.

There were several moments and experiences during my adolescence and young adult years that pushed me; however, the most significant of these was likely learning to accept and embrace my own queer identity. Once your eyes are opened to your own oppression, it becomes harder and harder to ignore or disbelieve the oppression stories of others. I always say racism and sexism and homophobia and transphobia and all of the various ways we as humans have found to avoid loving one another are first cousins. They're all related and connected, stemming from the same place in our hearts that chooses fear over compassion.

Getting to know myself as a queer woman from the age of twenty-four (now thirty-seven) was and continues to be a long road. Internalized homophobia is complicated. Relating to family and friends within the context of my newly understood identity was complicated. I've marched for my own rights, in the modern queer liberation movement—standing on the shoulders of important leaders like Marsha P. Johnson and Larry Kramer, Phyllis Lyon and Leslie Feinberg. This version of myself was finally starting to feel authentic, as if I had at last mustered up the autonomy to decide who I actually was rather than who I was told to be. But this wasn't the Emily my hometown had envisioned. I began making connections between my own story and stories I'd grown up hearing from people of color—stories that my hometown glazed over, dismissed, denied. My experiences, things I know to be true with regard to the othered parts of me, were also glazed over, dismissed, denied. The assuredness I had in the existence of my own obstacles solely because of my queer identity opened the door for me to understand and empathize with obstacles people of color face. Once I acknowledged that people of color do experience challenges because of their race, it was impossible not to recognize the existence of white supremacy.

Somewhere along my journey to a deeper level of enlightenment, I reconnected with Chase (I call him "Chase"; some of you might know him as "James")—a kid, as I remembered him. He was several years younger than me, someone I perceived to be a typical jockish kind of straight guy from Grand Saline. At this point in my adult life, I was eager to connect with other like-minded hometown folks. I worried that, in order to be who I am and speak my own truth, I'd have to completely leave behind my roots. No one would understand who I'd become, no one would see and affirm the injustice I'd witnessed. No one believed in the existence of white supremacy as a long-standing structure, continuing to contribute to the progress of white people on the backs of people of color.

During a social media interaction, I could tell right away that Chase was someone I wanted to know. He was doing the exact antiracism work I'd come to understand was necessary. And he was using our shared experiences being from Grand Saline to inform that work—to come from a place of familiarity with the darker corners of our world, that, at best, deny the existence of racism and, at worst, actively discriminate against nonwhite people.

I started to realize that I didn't have to leave behind the small-town gal inside of me, that I could actually use that experience to effect change, to put these fragmented pieces of myself back together in a way that could contribute to the undoing of white supremacy.

Of course, this was and is a process—a long one and one that is ongoing. I've learned that the dismantling of white supremacy as a system also requires dismantling white supremacy within myself—identifying and sitting with certain reactions and feelings that sometimes rise to the surface, reminding me how deeply embedded my own racism is.

Part of the work I've done on myself occurred while Chase and his team were filming *Man on Fire*. Chase asked if I would be willing to be interviewed, and I was more than eager to contribute to the work he was doing. Uncomfortable and sometimes unpleasant though it might be, I knew it was necessary to do my part to shine a light on structural racism. Although Texas women are often perceived as the "speak when spoken to" submissive types, I subscribe to the Ann Richards school of thought, which we all know means unapologetically speaking truth to power.

During the interview, a particular experience came to mind that I hadn't thought about in years. I don't remember exactly what question triggered it, but speaking on it pushed a button in me that I didn't know existed. I was a cheerleader all throughout middle and high school. I loved the whole experience—learning the cheers and dances, the fanfare and anticipation of pep rallies, leading my hometown in cheers under the Friday-night lights, being a real part of the tradition of Texas high school football. It remains one of my fondest Grand Saline memories.

An important piece of being a cheerleader in Grand Saline was pep-rally skits. We worked hard to put together entertainment for Grand Saline students and staff during the school day every Friday. Skits were generally intended to be funny, which was where I could really shine. My ability to shamelessly amuse and entertain made up for my unfortunately nonexistent toe-touch.

I can't recall exactly the point of the particular skit that came to mind; I only remember that we performed the same scenario repeatedly in different "styles." For example, I think one "style" might've been "hick" or "hillbilly," so we delivered our lines and acted as such—with an exaggerated country accent and delivery. The "style" that I now deeply regret was "ghetto style." I had a significant part in this portion of the skit; therefore, I spoke and acted with every insensitive trope of Black people you can think of. I distinctly remember saying, "He be hurt!" instead of, "He's hurt." That was my understanding of Black, "ghetto" culture. It never occurred to me how reductive this was. I didn't consider that my part in the skit contributed to a dangerous stereotype of Black people—suggesting that they're less educated, less civilized, and thus that they don't speak "properly." At that point in my life, I'd had only a handful of encounters with Black people, none of which had been personal relationships. I had no business impersonating them; Black people aren't characters.

Retelling this event to Chase and his team as an adult hit me like a ton of bricks. Though I'd been patting myself on the back for leaving behind the parts of Grand Saline culture that upheld white supremacy, I still had so much work to do. In order to truly leave behind my latent racism, I'd have to sit with the mistakes I'd made. I'd have to work through my own racist thoughts and behaviors in order to find redemption. And it wasn't pretty. And it still isn't. The further I go into this introspective work, the further I realize I have to go. And it may never end.

I don't share my experiences to laud myself as a recovering racist. I believe my own journey is a metaphor for the requisite work Grand Saline as a community must also do. Looking at oneself in the mirror, both individually and as a collective, is dirty work. It requires intense vulnerability, laborious accountability. But it's necessary. And it's worth it.

If I could speak to the folks in Grand Saline, I'd plead with them to do one thing—listen.

Salt of the Earth and *Man on Fire* are not meant to be received as judgment or condemnation. Most of us on Chase's side of the fence have real affection for Grand Saline. I know I do. I see so much good in this community. It's my home, it's where I come from, it made me the woman I am in many ways. I only want for it to be a place of love and of tolerance and of progress. I believe that Grand Saline, and countless towns with similar histories, hold great potential—the potential to acknowledge the problems in their history and work to make them right. It's possible.

I pray for Grand Saline. I pray that this community will see the strength and beauty in its own vulnerability, and also in accountability. I pray that this town will begin to understand its contributions to oppression and also see the path to redemption.

I pray for change.

Emily Erwin

ACKNOWLEDGMENTS

THERE ARE MANY FOLKS I need to acknowledge for their role in helping shape this book over the past seven years. First, I want to thank Brad Lucas, my dissertation chair, for his love and support. He was the first person to push me to write about Charles Moore, suggesting that maybe this story wouldn't be a chapter in my dissertation but should be my entire project. He had the vision to see the wider scope before I ever could. I will always be grateful for his advice. To the rest of my committee, Richard Enos, Charlotte Hogg, and Max Krochmal, thanks for your guidance during the dissertation project. It helped me see how I could play with the genre of this book. I am ever grateful to Charles Moore's family. Thank you for spending hours with me doing interviews and going through Charles's notes. The bonds we created will always be some of my most cherished. Shout-out to Terry Peterman, Joshua Daniel, Carrie Helms Tippen, and Tyler Shane Branson for reading and responding to various chapters. Y'all are the real ones. I am grateful that my family, Jan Smith, David and Ginger Smith, Rickey and Melanie Sanchez, and Chris and Halie Gaw, supported me unequivocally along the way. Y'all make me a better person. Special thanks to Victor Villanueva for the suggestion to break the narrative from the analysis and for helping me find my voice in the narrative. This book wouldn't be what it is without him. Also, I am grateful that Steve Parks and NCTE gave me the space to publish this research. When I first came to Steve with half of a book idea, he helped me imagine how it could be a full book idea. I can also say that much of this book couldn't exist without my film partner, Joel Fendelman, who believed that I could produce a documentary with no filmmaking experience. You shaped my career and passions, and I look forward to working with you for many years to come. Last, to my partner, Katie, I appreciate your listening when I needed to talk about the various ebbs and flows of this project. Listening will always be enough.

INTRODUCTION

> You are the salt of the earth. But if the salt loses its saltiness, how
> can it be made salty again? It is no longer good for anything,
> except to be thrown out and trampled underfoot.
>   —Matthew 5.13, New International Version

GRAND SALINE, TEXAS, ABOUT seventy miles east of Dallas, isn't known
for much.

A few decades ago the community had a storied football legacy
that eventually faded once the decorated head coach, Carter El-
liott, retired in the late 1990s. Though Grand Saline never won a
state title, they collected numerous divisional and regional playoff
victories and were even featured on MTV's *True Life* in 2001, in an
episode titled "I'm a Football Hero." The episode followed leaders
of two teams, Grand Saline and Celina, as they prepared for their
regional football playoff game and was a point of pride for people
in the town, even though Grand Saline lost the game. The veins of
the town's football legacy run deep, and its pride can still be felt in
the bleachers on most Friday evenings in the fall.

Chris Tomlin, a contemporary Christian music singer who won
a Grammy, hails from the town as well, but he isn't well-known
outside of people who listen to Christian worship music.

Perhaps the town is most well-known for the salt flats that rest
on the south side of the town—owned by the Morton Salt Company. The Morton Salt mine is one of the "purest" in all of America
(Harper), and locals claim that if you eat a salted pretzel anywhere
around the country, you have tasted salt that comes from Grand Saline (Sanchez, *Man on Fire*). From these flats, Grand Saline earned
its nickname, "The Salt of the Earth," which associates the town's
Christian roots with its largest industry.

"You are the salt of the earth," proclaims Jesus in Matthew 5.13,
noted in the epigraph. In this particular biblical tale, Jesus, sitting

on the mountainside, states to his audience that their goodness—their purity—is key to saving others. Being the salt of the earth can lead others to Christianity. Being pious, loving God, and living for God is what Jesus asks of his followers. However, if they lose that saltiness, if they lose their purity, they no longer have a purpose. They are no longer helping people. Jesus calls for Christians to be the salt of the earth.

However, salt has many functions.

Salt preserves.

The salt in Grand Saline's industry and name may not carry the same symbolic value as that of the Bible, but its symbolism still exists. The "purity" in Grand Saline is within the race of its people, or rather, the *whiteness* of the town. I define the term *whiteness* here as "a socially constructed category that is normalized within a system of privilege so that it is taken for granted by those who benefit from it" (Applebaum 402). So for people in Grand Saline, white systems of being (such as white culture, white appearance and clothes, and white ideologies) are privileged over systems of being that nonwhite people might embrace. While many East Texas towns have fully integrated and better represent the racial demographics of the state as a whole, Grand Saline stands out as exceptionally white. The town is slightly below state averages for its Latinx population, representing about 20 percent of the town, but it has less than a one percent Black population, which is significantly less than all other towns in the area (Dean 5A). I actually don't even know of a single Black family that lives in town. Other nearby communities, including Van, Edgewood, Canton, and Mineola, all have notable Black populations, and many of these Black people have heard racist stories about Grand Saline.

Historically, salt has been used to desiccate food. Salting dehydrates meat, creating an environment where cultures (especially bacteria and fungi) can't grow. The salt density stops anything from developing—or effectively kills it—via osmosis. Of course, I am not a food biologist or a scientist in the least, but I am intrigued by the way salt preserves because I see the saltiness of Grand Saline, its whiteness, also being preserved through what I will call a *rhetoric of white supremacy.* I will touch on this definition later, but for now, I want to stick with the metaphor. Just as placing dry salt on a piece of meat preserves its character through killing off living bacteria so does Grand Saline preserve its whiteness via particular rhetorical strategies—effectively "killing off" any sense of diversity, inclusion, or multiculturalism. The preservation of meat is an extension of life because without it diseases such as salmonella, listeria, or trichinosis might prosper. While the people of Grand Saline might consider their own rhetorical preservation of white supremacy as a good quality, many readers, I assume, will think differently. The town preserves its white culture not out of necessity for life but out of fear of a white cultural death, an unfounded fear that has existed within white communities for centuries.

Their salt preserves them but not from any real threat.

DEFINING WHITE SUPREMACY

Before I explain how a culture of white supremacy pervades Grand Saline, though, I need to define *white supremacy,* because that definition is pertinent to the arguments in this text. Historically and in popular culture, white supremacy has simply been defined as the ideologies and beliefs that white people are better than people of color. When the term *white supremacy* is invoked in contemporary society, most in the public might conjure images of the Ku Klux Klan, the Jim Crow South, or the Proud Boys (a new right-wing hate group that often promotes versions of explicit white power) (Wilson). As Carol Anderson states, historically, we have viewed white supremacy as being embodied in hate groups, supporters of hate groups, or people who hold openly racist views (such as "I hate wetbacks").

However, this trope has been transformed greatly in the twenty-first century. Critical race theorists have long stated that racism isn't static; it evolves (Beydoun). The same is true for white supremacy, a specific form of racism. Whereas historically it has been understood as an outward version of white superiority, it has been altered, rhetorically, to maintain power in contemporary society. I argue that we can better understand white supremacy today as *the ways in which people and institutions enact and reinforce ideologies of white superiority.* This definition includes overt forms of white supremacy—such as recent fliers from the Ku Klux Klan suggesting that a white genocide is happening in America (Campbell; Sanchez, "Trump")—to more tacit ones—such as people who argue that racism isn't a "big deal" today. This last example would be an act of white supremacy because it *reinforces* white superiority, subtly, by excusing unawareness of racism in the present.

Many readers will probably be able to name various acts that would encompass the ways white supremacy is enacted via people and institutions. Racist epithets, cultural racism, and displays of racial bias all are acts that are quite easy to name, and because we can qualify them as explicitly (or explicitly to some, at least) racist, they aren't as effective in a country that mostly decries such hatred (though, under Trump's regime, explicit racism seemed as much *en vogue* as ever). Yet what about being complicit with white supremacy? What about staying silent in the face of it? Telling stories that promote subjugation but can be framed as "jokes"? The ways identities are negotiated and performed in light of a racist culture? These might be more difficult to name because they are more covert and because they don't explicitly enact bigotry; rather, they support it. These acts keep the structure of white supremacy in place—they are the pillars on which overt white supremacy stands—and they are the central subjects for this book's inquiry.

I will be examining white supremacy by looking at the rhetorical practices within the culture of Grand Saline. Whereas a cursory understanding of my title might suggest that I am exploring explicit practices, instead I focus on the covert acts, the mechanisms that sustain, maintain, and preserve white supremacy in my hometown. The implicit ones are the building blocks for explicit white supremacy. They are the behaviors, ideologies, and identities that people learn in becoming white supremacists. If we are able to dismantle these practices, then we have the chance to topple the more egregious versions too. Overall, my definition of white supremacy makes clear connections between covert rhetorical practices and our understanding of white supremacy in the twenty-first century.

MEMORIES OF RACISM: THE STORIES OF GRAND SALINE, CHARLES MOORE, AND ME

People have been digging for salt in this East Texas area for centuries. Local Native American tribes used the salt flats to gather the mineral for years. Near the turn of the twentieth century, after Jordan's Saline (a mile southwest of Grand Saline) was founded, multiple salt mines controlled the town's economy. Morton Salt eventually bought out all competing companies and took over production in the 1920s and was the only salt company in newly founded Grand Saline by 1931 (Kleiner). While the town boomed relative to its region in the post-Reconstruction era, the Great Depression eventually left the community without an economy; the town never grew much past three thousand residents. Today Morton Salt is the largest employer in town (with around two hundred employees as of 2015). The downtown area looks like most other current East Texas towns, comprising decaying buildings, abandoned businesses, and other vestiges of the past. It appears lifeless. I attended middle school in Grand Saline for two years (from 2000 to 2002) before moving to the town during my high school years (2002 to 2006). I remember driving through the town on weekend nights when there was nothing else to do and would see reminders of what once was—the empty movie stores, salons, and restaurants that once promised growth and prosperity were now lost. Nothing has changed much in the fifteen years since I left.

But underneath the surface of this stagnant town lie racist depths, racism that has existed or been talked about for well over a century. Though most of the community would not refer to themselves as racist or white supremacist, locals from nearby towns, especially communities of color, would beg to differ. I would call it a "well-known secret," but it wasn't a secret at all. To grow up in Grand Saline is to grow up believing your community is more racist than other communities.

This is why on June 23, 2014, Charles Moore, an elderly white minister, self-immolated in the Family Dollar parking lot in Grand Saline—to protest the town's racism. In a letter he left on his car windshield, titled "O Grand Saline Repent of Your Racism" (see

Figures 1 and 2), he declared that he was born and raised in town and remembered the racist misdeeds of the community's past—lynchings, hangings, and stories of the Ku Klux Klan. He believed the town had never moved past its racist history. Moore's death mostly went unnoticed; local and regional news did not even name him until ten days after the incident (Dean; Repko).

O GRAND SALINE, REPENT OF YOUR RACISM

I was born in Grand Saline, Texas almost 80 years ago. As I grew up, I heard the usual racial slurs, but they didn't mean much to me. I don't remember even meeting an African-American person until I began driving a bus to Tyler Junior College and made friends with the mechanic who cared for the vehicles: I teased him about his skin-color, and he became very angry with me: that is one way I learned about the pain of discrimination.

During my second year as a college student, I was serving a small church in the country near Tyler, when the United States Supreme Court declared racial discrimination in schools illegal in 1954; when I let it be known that I agreed with the Court's ruling, I was cursed and rejected. When word about that got back to First Methodist Church in Grand Saline (which had joyfully recommended me for ministry—the first ever from the congregation), I was condemned and called a Communist; during the 60 years since then, I have never once been invited to participate in any activity at First Methodist (except family funerals), let alone to speak from its pulpit.

When I was about 10-years-old, some friends and I were walking down the road toward the creek to catch some fish, when a man called "Uncle Billy" stopped us and called us into his house for a drink of water—but his real purpose was to cheerily tell us about helping to kill "niggers" and put their heads up on a pole. A section of Grand Saline was (maybe still is) called "pole town," where the heads were displayed. It was years later before I knew what the name meant.

During World War II, when many soldiers came through town on the train, the citizens demanded that the shades in the passenger cars be pulled down if there were African-Americans aboard, so they wouldn't have to look at them.

The Ku Klux Klan was once very active in Grand Saline, and still probably has sympathizers in the town. Although it is illegal to discriminate against any race relative to housing, employment, etc., African-Americans who work in Grand Saline live elsewhere. It is sad to think that schools, churches, businesses, etc. have no racial diversity when it comes to blacks.

My sense is that most Grand Saline residents just don't want black people among them, and so African-Americans don't want to live there and face rejection. This is a shame that has bothered me wherever I went in the world, and did not want to be identified with the town written up in the newspaper in 1993, but I have never raised my voice or written a word to contest the situation. I have owned my old family home at 1212 N. Spring St. for the last 15 years, but have never discussed the issue with my tenants.

Since we are currently celebrating the 50th anniversary of Freedom Summer in 1964, when people started working in the South to attain the right to vote for African-Americans along with other concerns. This past weekend was the anniversary of the murder of three young men (Goodman, Schwerner and Cheney) in Philadelphia, Mississippi, which gave great impetus to the Civil Rights Movement—since this historic time is being remembered, I find myself very concerned about the rise of racism across the country at the present time. Efforts are being made in many places to make voting more difficult for some people, especially African-Americans. Much of the opposition to President Obama is simply because he is black.

I will soon be eighty years old, and my heart is broken over this. America (and Grand Saline prominently) have never really repented for the atrocities of slavery and its aftermath. What my hometown needs to do is open its heart and its doors to black people, as a sign of the rejection of past sins.

Figure 1. A copy of Charles Moore's letter to Grand Saline.

Figure 2. The cover of the letter Moore left behind for family.

I heard about Moore's death moments after he lit the flame because multiple people on my social media feeds posted about it. After I read his powerful words and understood his vision, I became aware of my own truth: If I ever had one story to tell, it was the story of Charles Moore. From there, I wrote my dissertation on Moore's act and the rhetoric of self-immolation globally and produced a documentary titled *Man on Fire*, which premiered on PBS, as a part of *Independent Lens*, on December 17, 2018. The film tracks the final moments of Charles Moore's life and investigates the legacy of racism in Grand Saline. Studying Moore's life taught me a lot about myself. I felt a certain kinship in understanding our parallel views of racism in Grand Saline (we both felt that the town must publicly attempt to move past its racist culture rather than continually deny it), and reading his sermons reminded me very much of my grandfather, who was a Southern Baptist preacher in a nearby community.

Moore was a passionate person. He fought for integration in East Texas in the 1950s and was asked to leave a church because of his progressive racial ideologies (Hall, "Man on Fire"). He traveled to Chicago in the height of the Civil Rights Movement to fight for the cause and lived in India for two years in the 1970s for a mission trip. In 1996, by the time he lived in Austin and had a new church, he went on a fifteen-day hunger strike to protest the United Methodist Church's stance on LGBTQ+ issues during the denomination's national conference held in Austin (Ward, "Methodist Minister"). His action helped persuade the convention to change their stance (Ward, "Austin Minister"). Moore was also a terrific writer and preacher who always inspired and challenged his parishioners. In one well-known sermon, "Lazarus, Come Out!" he ponders in closing: "Is it not we who have bound gay and lesbian persons with graveclothes . . . of hateful rules and sanctimonious customs, and tried to embalm them with sweet-odored salves of pious shibboleths, all the while singing exalted hymnodies about the immutable divine virtues of the traditional family?" His progressive stances intertwined with his faith. In another sermon, Moore denounced the hatred for the impoverished across the country, especially from those calling themselves Christians. He concludes:

> Yet—in spite of all the demeaning of poor persons, the justifications for being well-off, the platitudes about self-help, the cynicism about government and even the protests over my preaching a sermon having to do with a great injustice happening in our political system—when all this is said and done, the spirit of Jesus, full of compassion and common sense, will constantly confront us, saying: You give them something to eat. ("You Give Them Something to Eat")

Moore's life greatly affected my own because his passion for social justice, his willingness to fight for his beliefs, and the love and compassion he spread in his sermons mirrored my own views and ideologies. I still think of him almost every single day.

However, after producing the film and writing my dissertation, I knew that my work on Grand Saline wasn't over. Though I had spent dozens of hours in the archives, examining Grand Saline's racial past, and hours interviewing historians from around the Grand Saline area, something was missing. Though I interviewed over sixty-five people during the dissertation and film process, my understanding of Grand Saline was not complete. I realized, finally, that I had never considered myself in relation to my hometown— How had I participated in racism and also been a victim of it? How had my relationship to Grand Saline changed after I left and after Moore's self-immolation? What impact did making *Man on Fire* have on the town's views of me and my view of the town? When I considered how much had changed from starting my dissertation in 2014 to completing the dissertation and film in 2017 and 2018, I realized there was still an unexplored variable: myself.

I am entrenched within the town's story of white supremacy.

My identity stems from how I was treated in Grand Saline. I told racist stories and legends. I participated in the town's white supremacist culture. I knew all the tales and histories. Yet, even as I participated in racism, my nicknames were still "Wetback" and "Beaner." I was stuck in between being a racist participant and being a racist target.

However, as I began the dissertation and film, I also became entangled in the story of my hometown in a different way—as someone trying to change the town's culture. I was critiqued for talking about racism openly, for "race-baiting," and for being a "traitor." I challenged people's racial ideologies privately and publicly. As one interviewee told me, "Everyone in town reads your Facebook page . . . and knows that you are wrong." I am not only a product of the white supremacist culture in Grand Saline; I am the face of activists attempting to change it.

My book uses personal stories from my middle school and high school experiences to discuss the way Grand Saline constructs racial identity and forces assimilation and how stories of historical racism are communicated to insiders and outsiders. I also talk about the filmmaking experience, in which I was lead producer and interviewer for *Man on Fire*. This role made me the most prominent "outside agitator" for many in Grand Saline (besides, perhaps, Charles Moore himself), as my duties included securing interviews with people (a tough task), conducting the interviews, and helping piece the story together during postproduction. I was fortunate to work with an amazing director, Joel Fendelman, on this project and am ever grateful that he trusted me to be lead producer. Some of the incidents that occurred while producing this film also make up this text.

Overall, my book is composed of my own memories, textual analysis, and the interviews of sixty-five people. Interviewees discussed Charles Moore, Grand Saline's history, and racial issues within the community. While some of the interviewees were Grand Saline residents, others were former residents, and a few were white people and people of color from neighboring communities. My book employs many of these interviews not to extrapolate any quantifiable information about the town but rather to illustrate themes in how these people discuss issues of racism, whiteness, and the town's legacy.

RESEARCH QUESTIONS AND CHAPTER OUTLINE

As noted above, I define white supremacy as the ways in which people and institutions enact and reinforce ideologies of white superiority, and while this definition is important for the arguments of this text, my text does not explicitly work to build this definition. Rather, I attempt to understand the rhetorical components that *maintain* white supremacy. If we understand that racism and white supremacy evolve in order to keep whiteness at the top of the racial hierarchy, then we must understand how that evolution rhetorically functions. What does white supremacy in rural America look like today, especially a white supremacy that isn't explicit? How does it subjugate people of color? How does it indoctrinate white people and minorities? How might we not only see it but be able to critique it? How does it force assimilation, influence storytelling, and silence others? This book attempts to answer these questions through my case study of Grand Saline.

My analysis is thus informed by autoethnographic and cultural-rhetorics methodologies. I use these methodologies for a few different reasons. First, at my core, I am a storyteller. A good story can effectively share knowledge and research just as well as traditional scholarship can (I'm thinking of Victor Villanueva's *Bootstraps*, Keith Gilyard's *Voices of the Self*, and most of Aja Martinez's work). Also, in thinking about the white supremacy in my hometown, it would feel less authentic to focus on the stories of others but not my own. Since one of my central claims is that I was a part of

this white supremacist tradition as much as anyone else, my stories provide the space to talk about my "personal lived experiences
and their relationship to culture," which is Robin M. Boylorn and
Mark P. Orbe's definition of autoethnography. Last, I view my approach as an extension of a cultural-rhetorics orientation, an orientation based upon "all the meaning-making practices and their
relationships" (Powell et al.).

My work attempts to better understand—to constellate—the
meaning-making practices of white supremacy in my hometown
and how they create relationships between town members, between
Grand Saline residents and residents of other towns, and between
me and members of my home community. The stories I tell and
my subsequent analyses of them focus on these relationships and
attempt to pinpoint epistemologies of white supremacy.

To do this, I investigate the town with an autoethnographic and
cultural-rhetorics lens. I focus on three functions: *assimilation, hegemonic storytelling*, and *silencing* as rhetorical moves the community uses to *preserve* white supremacy. In the seven chapters I outline
below, I use three, Chapters 1, 3, and 5, to tell my stories about my
experiences in Grand Saline. Chapter 1 focuses on stories of how I
found my racial identity and assimilated into whiteness and white
supremacy in my community. Chapter 3 highlights the racist storytelling traditions I learned, repeated, and constructed during my
middle school and high school days. Chapter 5 centers on Moore's
self-immolation and the creation and public airing of my film project—to emphasize silencing as a rhetorical tactic. Between these
chapters, I provide analyses of the narratives themselves. Chapter 2
focuses on the rhetoric of white supremacist assimilation, Chapter
4 on racist storytelling, and Chapter 6 on the rhetoric of silencing.
Finally, Chapter 7 explores how Grand Saline might change and
details my concluding promise to the community.

However, before closing, I want to untangle my relationship
with Grand Saline. As a kid, I loved my time in town (even while
participating in the town's white supremacy on a seemingly daily
basis) and still have fond, nonracist memories there. This book is
not meant to disparage Grand Saline or vilify the community. I am

still friends with many people I went to high school with—some who are actively working to correct white supremacist issues and others who are not—and affectionately remember their families' love and care. I do not deny or erase any of that. Nonetheless, I also cannot deny my other memories—memories of racism—many of which make up this book. This book is not written out of hatred or a misguided scholarly vision; it comes from my love and desire to turn to action, to help Grand Saline and myself by acknowledging the truth.

Salt conserves meat.

It maintains food.

And the "salt" of Grand Saline—the town's whiteness—preserves too. It preserves white supremacy.

This book exists in order to label it, challenge it, and, I hope, change it.

1

Whoosh

I STARTED SCHOOL IN Grand Saline in 2001, when I was in seventh grade, because I wanted a better education—or at least that was the pretense for moving. In reality, my sister was finishing her senior year of high school in Alba (ten miles north of Grand Saline) and had suffered multiple bad encounters with the principal/dictator-in-residence there, and my mother didn't want me to deal with similar harassment. Personally, I had a better reason for changing school. I was already close to six feet tall and was gifted at football because of my size. Alba was terrible at all sports, but Grand Saline had a reputation for making deep football playoff runs. So I transferred to the middle school and eventually moved to the town in ninth grade.

Before my mom, (eventually former) stepdad, and I made this decision, though, we watched the episode of MTV's *True Life* that featured the Grand Saline football program. The show built up these high schoolers as gods—men prepared to take the football field in honor of their town and their football tradition. Unfortunately, Grand Saline lost the game, but they earned a new sense of pride that they could share with the local community, a community delighted by the fact that their school was respected on national television. They also gained something else after this episode aired—the devotion of a young kid only a few miles north of the town. I watched these guys and had an innate desire to join in their legacy, to become the pride of a community like those ahead of me.

I arrived at the school early in the fall of 2001 and immediately joined the football team. Being the new kid in a small school with students who have all grown up with one another can be tough, especially when having the last name Sanchez and being browner than most of your peers (there were probably about fifteen Mexican Americans in our grade, making up 20 percent of the class).

Still, I fit right in.

I think this is partly because I had a certain larger-than-life demeanor. I am a people person by nature, but I was also a kid in essentially a man's body, which meant I was good at football. In a culture that labeled football as king, it is good to be the biggest and most athletic body on the field. That year our football team went undefeated. We beat a few schools in larger divisions and had only one close game.

As we moved into eighth grade with some swagger, districts realigned and a tougher game was added to our schedule: the team from Winona, a town about thirty miles east of Grand Saline. Winona has fewer people than Grand Saline and does not have the same football legacy; however, they had a quarterback who was just as good a runner as he was a passer.

He was also Black.

We knew that our eighth-grade district championship would come down to this game, as we were both undefeated late in the season. During the week leading up to our matchup, we kept hearing from our coaches about how tough this quarterback would be on the field. In one practice, a coach placed our fastest teammate at quarterback so we could better understand what sort of runner we would be facing. "Well, their quarterback is obviously darker than Randy,"[1] our coach chuckled. "But their quarterback is just as fast, if not faster." The team laughed along with the coach—believing his comments about the opposing player's skin color to be funny. Since there were no Black people living in Grand Saline, Black people were often the butt of racist jokes. It was—and still is—part of the town's culture. Sure, it was odd to hear an authority figure make such a comment, but students didn't know how to respond. It was acceptable—even preferred—to make such jokes. Coaches and elders in the community joined in the practice as well.

On a Thursday evening in the fall, we drove forty-five minutes east to Winona for the game. While the seventh-grade team was finishing their contest on the field, we stood in one of the end zones doing our stretches to warm up. Oftentimes, coaches would lead us in these warm-ups, keeping our stretches homogenized and motivating us, but they weren't watching over us on this particular occasion. A couple of my friends and I stood in the end zone, stretching, while looking across the field at our opponents doing the same calisthenics. As young boys, we believed this routine would intimidate the other team before the game. (It did nothing.)

One of my teammates leaned in close to me and said something explicitly racist and anti-Black.[2]

My other friend jumped in, "Don't say that to Chase. He's Brown." (When I was a kid, I went by Chase, my middle name. I am still known as Chase to many of my friends, but I also go by James in professional settings.)

"Being Brown isn't the same as being Black," the first teammate retorted.

I stretched in silence, trying to focus on the game ahead of us, but I couldn't shake a weird feeling. I had never focused much on my race or ethnicity before, but to hear someone calling me "Brown"—and how that was different from being "Black"—made me feel, well, different. However, I knew I couldn't focus on that difference in this moment. I was a part of a team, and we had a goal to accomplish.

We went on to beat Winona that evening in a close game. The quarterback was tough, and he singlehandedly kept the game close, but we overwhelmed them with our power. We weren't as fast as this team, but we were much stronger, and for thirteen- and fourteen-year-old kids that makes a big difference. So while Winona's quarterback was able to slip past us a few times for touchdowns, we were able to overpower their defense just a bit more. Yet there was something else in the air that night. Maybe we felt as if we were on the precipice of greatness. The fans seemed a bit louder and more attuned to our every move. All the players seemed a bit more motivated to win, more inspired in the huddles and more focused, and that evidently made the difference. Was it because this would be for the district title? Or was it something else?

After the game I found my family on the sidelines, per custom. Though many of my family members attended my games, I always sought out my grandfather, a 6'5" man who, legend has it, was once invited by the Dallas Cowboys to try out for the team (though I never saw any official paperwork, my family swears by this legend), because he would give me pointers. I trusted his advice more than anyone's—more than even my coaches'. Most of the time he would positively reinforce my play ("Remember that block you had on that third and seven in the third quarter?"), but he could criticize too ("Y'all would have scored sooner had you blocked that linebacker five yards up field!"). However, this evening, instead of giving me advice or affirming my play on the field, my grandfather had something else on his mind.

"Chase, follow me. I have someone I want you to meet." He turned around and started walking.

I followed behind him as we moved from the visitor sidelines to the home stands. Why would we go to the opponent's sidelines? In front of me, he was talking to my grandma about something that excited him. I could hear certain words, "neighbor" and "years," but I was too absorbed in our victory to listen. Finally, we approached an older Black couple, and he introduced me to them. "They used to live right next door to me and your grandma when we lived here a few decades ago. And this is their grandson!" I shook their hands as they congratulated me on the win and moved toward their grandson—the Winona quarterback—who lingered in the background.

As our grandparents reminisced for a few minutes, I gazed into the quarterback's eyes and felt an immense shame—shame in knowing that some of my teammates had referred to him with a racist epithet, shame for not saying anything to my teammates, and shame in knowing that I was different too, though I couldn't name why. I wanted to apologize to him and wanted to forget everything my teammates had talked about at the beginning of the game.

His eyes spoke back, too. He knew what my football team and community thought of him. He knew the racism we harbored. He knew.

I lived in two different houses in Grand Saline with my single mother. They were side by side. During my ninth-grade year, we moved from Alba into a small house in town that couldn't have been more than eight hundred square feet. However, when my sister got in a car accident and had to move back in with us during the summer before my eleventh-grade year, we relocated to the house next door (same landlord), which was substantially larger. It was probably only thirteen hundred square feet, but that was big to me.

My mother wasn't home much because she commuted an hour each way for work, so I would see her when I woke up in the mornings and around 6:30 each evening. My sister, who was in and out of college, was in and out of the house, too. I'm not sure if this made me independent or if that was just my nature, but I could take care of myself. It was necessary. Still, even though our living situation was less than ideal, I found comfort in an odd phenomenon that occurred because of our place, something that wasn't very comforting when I first moved to town: the *whoosh* of the speeding train on the railroad tracks only a block away from me.

When we first moved to the area, I hated the *whoosh*. The train horn would blare from miles away, and the train would sweep by the house intermittently throughout the day, reminding everyone of the sheer velocity at which sound can travel. It was worse during the night. During my first few weeks living in town, the horn would wake me from my sleep, alarming me with the presence of an intruder in the background. Later, the intruder became a friend, a comforting sensation. Especially the *whoosh* that would happen when the train approached the house—with the horn gaining in intensity—and finally passing us and drowning out into the night. That sound was home. Even if it woke me in the middle of the night, it still gave me peace, the comfort of a noise reminding you that you are safe.

However, the train and tracks have a more symbolic meaning in Grand Saline. While the town was not fully segregated, it still had major divides by class and ethnicity. The railroad track that ran parallel to the major highway in the town (running east and west) was the dividing point for this segregation. Most of the Mexican

Americans and poorest people lived on the south side of the tracks—many of the houses were small and run-down, and one of the neighborhoods was called "Poletown," or "Po' Town" for short (more on this later). There was no certainty that if you were poor or Brown you lived on this side of the track, but it was definitely true for most. The people on the north side of the tracks were by no means rich—there aren't many upper-class citizens in the town— but they were generally better-off and whiter.

I lived a block north of the tracks. With my white mother. And my somewhat Brown body. And my lack of Spanish. And a lack of wealth. I was on the line, but nonetheless I was on the "right" (or "white") side of the tracks. I embodied this complex identity.

Even though I was someone at the intersection of segregation, my popularity hid my identity issues. Maybe it was that I was "Brown" but not *Brown* to my white peers. I truly didn't fit in with either the white crowd (being that my last name is Sanchez—pronounced *San*-chez—and my skin tone is still a bit darker than the most sun-kissed, tanned white skin) nor the Brown crowd (being that I didn't speak Spanish, my mom was white, and I didn't have the same cultural knowledge).

But I was smart. My "intelligence" taught me to associate with the white kids. I believed I more closely aligned with them. We all enjoyed the same things—American football, beer, and partying. I never consciously associated with the white kids because of their race, but I think I did choose them because it was easy. I could more readily assimilate into Grand Saline and the culture of the town if I chose whiteness.

However, whiteness didn't always choose me.

During high school, I "dated" a white girl, Elizabeth, for a few months. She was nice and smart and fun, and since I hadn't done much dating before, this experience was fairly new for me. After a few weeks of going out, I went to her house one Friday evening to eat dinner with her family and watch movies. Since Grand Saline is such a small community, there wasn't much to do on the weekends—eating with families and watching movies was a culturally accepted "date" unless we wanted to go out and party.

I was not too nervous to sit down with her family. Her mother, Debbie, cooked spaghetti and had a beautiful dining table set for the five of us: my date, her mom, her dad, her brother, and me. We passed around the salad and pasta while talking. I told her family about my eventual college plans and my goals in life: becoming an author (my ambitions haven't changed too much). They smiled and talked about their own writing ventures. As we finished eating, Debbie left the room to get dessert, and the conversation shifted away from ambitions in life to family. Mark, my date's father, told me that his family had only lived in the town for a few generations, but they were happy to be in a safe community. He had lived in a larger city earlier in life and had always hated feeling afraid.

He turned to me, "How long have you lived in Grand Saline?"

"Well," I replied. "I have only lived here for a few years. I lived in Alba before moving here."

"Oh, yeah? Where is your family from?"

"My mom's family moved all around Texas during much of her life but her mom is from Van [ten miles south of Grand Saline], and her dad is from Edgewood [ten miles west of Grand Saline]."

"I meant your Sanchez side. Where are they from?"

"They all live an hour south of here in Tyler."

"But they aren't *from here*, are they?"

It was then that I had the cultural awareness to understand what Mark was asking, even in my adolescence.

"I am only 25 percent Mexican," I replied quickly, trying to not make eye contact with him. My eyes darted toward my girlfriend but she was chatting with her brother. "My dad's mom is from Tyler, but my grandfather immigrated from Mexico when he was a young kid."

And then Mark asked the only "logical" question: "Did he do so legally?"

I felt extremely uncomfortable in that situation. No one should have to defend their family's heritage and status in a country, and as a kid, talking to an adult, I felt even more uncertain of how to defend myself. This question made me feel different from Mark and his family. They never got asked about heritage. Or if they did, it was a point of pride being from some Western European country probably. Telling him part of my family was from Mexico made me feel as if I was admitting a dirty secret, something I should be ashamed of. Even if Mark felt comfortable having me in his house and feeding me, he still viewed me as "other." My skin, my heritage, would always be a question to him.

I looked down at the table as Debbie came into the room with pie. I felt embarrassed to answer. "He came here legally," I said quietly. Mark dropped the subject as Debbie began to fill our plates. I didn't date Elizabeth for much longer.

Even with all the racial issues in high school—figuring out where I stood and who was like me—I still had good grades. No one could take my intelligence away from me—even if I didn't always use it. I hardly ever attempted to earn all As in my classes and was known as a slacker. Nonetheless, I could always make the good grades without trying. The product of a broken academic system that had teachers teaching to the test and not really caring about what their students learned, I knew how to get by. I knew the coaches clearly didn't care about teaching, and I could just focus on the workbooks in class and not listen to anything they said. If I didn't have to study to earn good grades, why would I ever try? I think my slacking attitude made people perceive me as someone who would never care about his educational future.

During the early parts of my senior year, I began thinking about college with my mom and my family. It was always the plan for me to attend college, but we didn't have any money saved up and were looking for scholarships and other grants that could help me attend school. My mom had gone to college for a few years and dropped out. My dad had gone back later in life. I had other family members who had graduated with various degrees (even one earning his doctorate in medicine), but I wasn't close enough with any of them to ask for advice. We didn't have the resources that we should have had. So one day I set a meeting with my guidance counselor to talk about the prospects of higher education.

I think I understood what guidance counselors looked like at other schools—or maybe I just imagined them a certain way because of movies and TV shows. They're someone you are supposed to talk with about your education, your future, and potentially your problems. They're always helpful and know how to solve the toughest of problems. That's not what a guidance counselor looked like at my small school. I never really remember ever chatting with this person about anything before entering her office one day in the fall.

I went to her office that day with an A- grade average, a middle-of-the-road SAT score, and a fair number of extracurricular activities on my transcript. I could have attended most of the nonprestigious universities in Texas, but I only know this now because I am a professor. Eighteen-year-old me had no idea what college would look like. I entered the guidance counselor's office and sat in one of two chairs in front of her desk. Her office was littered with those terrible motivational posters that everyone mocks (you know, the ones that define TEAMWORK or ACHIEVEMENT in clichés), and she seemed uncertain about what kind of conversation we would be having. A few of my friends had already discussed their college options with her, so I know this was a conversation she knew how to handle well, but at this moment she just seemed uncertain about the nature of my visit.

"Hi, Chase, what can I help you with today?" she asked. She was at her computer, still checking her email, only partly paying attention.

"Well, I know it's about time to start applying to colleges. I have a few ideas that I'd like to discuss with y . . . "

"Wait, you are thinking about college?" she seemed perplexed. Her eyes finally dashed away from the screen.

"Yes, I mean, of course. It has always been the next step."

"Oh. Well. Okay. I just thought you would have to go off to work. Nonetheless, I am glad that you came to see me. . . . "

The rest of the conversation went as well as it could have gone, I guess. I had received letters from some good colleges about the prospects of playing football for them. But we didn't talk about that. We talked about the junior college right down the road from me.

Why did she assume I would immediately work? It's true that many people in my hometown did go straight to the oilfield or other jobs—sometimes out of necessity but often for the lucrative wages—but they often didn't have my GPA. Most of them are white. I can't help thinking about the racial and socioeconomic undertones of this conversation because though maybe 25 percent or 33 percent of my graduating class were Mexican Americans, we were poorer than our white peers, and I would guess only a couple of us went to college. We were rare for our ethnic group. Would she have said this to another student who had my profile but was white?

Today the letters I have from some of these more prestigious schools hide in a box I have stored away in my spare bedroom. I look at them every time I move. Would life have been different with these other schools? Would I have been committed to my undergraduate education at these schools? Would I have been more prepared for graduate school? I am happy and fortunate to be where I am now, but it doesn't stop me from questioning. Ultimately, I am still upset that I didn't get a choice in the college decision making. The counselor chose my path for me.

However, I did have agency in other choices I made in high school—choices that still haunt me.

In Texas, race and ethnicity are often intertwined with language, especially in high school. To be Brown was to be less than. To have Spanish as your primary language was to be even lesser. I know this is true because most of the people who migrated to our high school and who were native Spanish-speakers were at the center of many jokes.[3] The worse one's English, the easier one was to ridicule. During my first or second year of school, a new student, Pablo, arrived in Grand Saline. His family had emigrated from Mexico, and there were serious questions among the students about whether he was "illegal or not." This issue of legality existed solely around the fact that he didn't speak much English; the Brazilian student in our class who was more fluent in English was never challenged on issues of legality.

I didn't have many classes with Pablo, but we had physics together in the afternoons.

This class, like many in my high school, wasn't remotely challenging. So I spent most of class time joking around with my friends and actively not paying attention to the lesson plan. When Pablo moved to the school, I found someone else to join me in shenanigans. He had broken English, and we didn't often understand each other, but we became friends through our mutual refusal to listen to our teacher. His refusal maybe stemmed from the language barrier, but we nonetheless bonded through this experience.

One day our teacher was absent and our school was unable to find a substitute, so the principal decided to put two science classes together (we were just working on our textbook problems, anyway). I found some seats near my close friends, my football buddies, and we immediately started disrespecting our substitute and not doing our work.

"So what's up with the new guy? Is he cool?" one of my friends asked.

"Yeah, he's funny, but he doesn't speak very much English, so we don't always understand one another."

"He doesn't speak English?" my friend asked, rhetorically, purposely misconstruing my words to imply that failure to understand some English meant *all* English.

He turned to Pablo, who was at a different table across the room, and started to speak in fake, broken gibberish that sounded more like an Asian dialect than anything remotely Spanish (being even more explicitly racist). My three friends and I laughed. I knew Pablo sensed the degradation, but he joined in the laughter too. He masked the pain.

I failed to speak out during this encounter. I did nothing. I could have told my friends this was wrong. I could have told a teacher. I could have gone to Pablo and apologized for my and my friends' transgressions. But I did nothing except partake in the "joke." I had agency to stand up for Pablo and call out racist bullshit, and I completely failed to stand up for him.

My silence preserved white supremacy as the norm and told Pablo that even other people of color will not stand up for him if it makes them uncomfortable. Though I did not actively participate in the hatred—I didn't openly mock Pablo—I still socially benefited from the white supremacy. I laughed because it made me part of the group. I was tangentially white.

Our relationship changed in that moment. Pablo and I could still joke around with each other in our class time together, but we never interacted outside of those moments. Maybe our friendship never would have blossomed, or maybe I was too embarrassed, or maybe he was upset at the cruel racism, but from then on, we were just acquaintances in a class that neither of us cared about.

Fast-forward fifteen years, and things are different in regard to my home . . . but also the same.

I now live in Vermont, a state that is 97 percent white. I work at Middlebury College, an elite small liberal arts school, which has its own racial issues (thanks, Charles Murray[4]). I have all sorts of privilege that come with living in New England, earning a good income, and having a secure job.

I still feel out of place, though, even while understanding the absolutely fortunate circumstances that led me to my job and my place. Maybe that's the thing. Maybe the discomfort is a part of my identity now. Maybe I am always at the edge of the divide, always lingering beside the train tracks wherever I am.

Sometimes, when I wake up in the middle of the night because I am thirsty or need to use the bathroom or am still processing some anxiety, I hear something outside of my apartment, in the far distance.

The train's *whoosh* calls me home.

2

The In-Between

> I am in between. . . . It is another borderland I inhabit. Not quite
> here nor there. On good days I feel I am a bridge. On bad days
> I just feel alone.
>
> —Sergio Troncoso

ALL OF THE STORIES IN THE previous chapter are about white supremacy to various degrees—showing me either being an agent for it (in
being silent and accepting it) or being a product of it (in never being "white" like my peers). These are stories about white supremacy,
but they are also about my own identity. They are about me trying
to assimilate into whiteness and bigotry.

Before I rhetorically analyze some of these encounters to better understand how whiteness and white supremacy influenced my
upbringing—and also how the rhetoric of assimilation was intertwined with these experiences—it's important to understand how I
choose to identify racially.

I am only a quarter Mexican American, I am browner than most
white folks and whiter than most Brown folks, I don't speak Spanish, I was raised by my white mom.

What am I?

Well, the United States Census—assumed to be the leading
data point for demographics in the United States—says that racial
choices for Americans are white; Black or African American; American Indian or Alaska Native; Asian; or Native Hawaiian or other
Pacific Islander. The census website says, "People who identify their
origin as Hispanic, Latino, or Spanish may be of any race." This
is because Brown isn't a race and people from "Brown" countries,

or Latinx countries, can be any race—some as white as any other white person and some as Black as any other Black person. Brown, in its very essence, is in-between: between races, between colors, between identities.

In this liminal state, I choose to be Chicanx.

In their book *Viva la Raza*, Yolanda Alaniz and Megan Cornish define *Chicano* as such: a term "used to designate all US-born or long-term US residents of Mexican origin, as distinguished from *recent* Mexican immigrants" (24). I select this term politically and for various reasons. First, I identify this way because it honors the tradition of the Chicanx Movement in the United States—the history of Chicanx and Filipino fieldworkers in California who went on strike for labor rights (Chávez). I use the term to respect these ancestors who fought for their right to be in the United States and to be treated as equals (even though we still aren't equal today). I also choose this term as a means to connote my own heritage. My Brown paternal grandfather emigrated from Mexico when he was a small child in the middle of the twentieth century, and he eventually married a white woman. I am only a quarter Mexican American—but that quarter blood is the lens I have for the world. With the last name Sanchez, it is hard for me to pass as "white." At best, I am racially ambiguous, and in that ambiguity I have more connection to my Brown brethren and sistren than to my white counterparts. Last, I think *Chicanx* accurately depicts who I am—part Mexican, part American. Just because I am more "American" than "Mexican" doesn't mean I am too "American" to be Chicanx. I am in-between, which is exactly what the term *Chicanx* signifies. Roberto Rodriguez writes that this term is born out of the need for a "self-definition" and that is how I intentionally use it (1).

However, this identity wasn't as clear to me as an adolescent. I was stuck between my racial and ethnic identities—stuck between racial groups, social classes, and the railroad tracks. I felt like no matter what the situation was I had to assimilate into different groups.

The history of race in the United States is the history of assimilation.

As critical race theorists Richard Delgado and Jean Stefancic note, scholars of race have differing views on whether nonwhite peoples should take a nationalist or assimilationist approach to living in the United States (60). In his article "Beyond the Rhetoric of Assimilation and Cultural Pluralism," Bill Ong Hing writes that many of these views of assimilation are uniquely tied to immigration, but there are "cultural-based objections" as well—moving past explicit racist claims and moving to implicit ones about language and cultural codes (874–75). Assimilation rhetoric has always been centered on whiteness, the idea that all language practices, grammar, cultural views, religious views, and even appearance should center on the culture of white people. There are many debates about how racialized people should respond to assimilation: Should they completely conform? Should they take a cultural-pluralist approach in which cultural minorities maintain their unique identities and, ideally, are accepted into broader society (Young; Kallen)? Should they be separatists? While these are important discussions and debates, they are not the emphasis of this chapter or this book. Assimilation wasn't a choice for me. It was the only option. Thus, I will be emphasizing the rhetoric that *made* me assimilate.

Aja Martinez writes about this extensively from a rhetorical perspective in describing the ways minorities "perform" assimilation in order to get into college, emphasizing how we give up our own culture in many ways to fit into the system ("'The American Way,'" 585). In her article "Alejandra Writes a Book," she also expresses this problem of assimilation in discussing graduate school and how she was told she "wasn't a 'good fit'" for a specific doctoral degree (59). To Martinez, the problem of assimilation stems from institutional performance—many gatekeepers (often white, elitist agents) have their visions for who and what does and does not count in representing specific institutions, and they want minority bodies to "fit" into their narrow perspectives. In *Bootstraps*, Victor Villanueva admits his own successes and failures in assimilating into higher education: "I have never stopped trying to assimilate. And I have succeeded in all the traditional ways. Yet complete assimilation is

denied—the Hispanic English professor. One can't get more culturally assimilated and still remain other" (xiv). Both Martinez's
and Villanueva's personal narratives emphasize the ways they had
to rhetorically change themselves—their language practices, their
writing, their interactions—in order to fit into a system that sometimes recognized them as equals but often did not.

Still, in this question of assimilation and whiteness, I am not
the only Chicanx person who has ever aligned with whiteness (and
thus white supremacy), and research illustrates the reasons that
individuals identify this way. Some point to economic pressures
(Wilkinson); others point to prominent positions and political
power (Harris) understandings of racial hierarchies (Frank et al.),
and resistance to Blackness (Darity et al.). However, it is Betina
Cutaia Wilkinson who I believe best summarizes my own position:
"Latinos' perceptions of closeness with a group are moderated by
their sense of influence. When Latinos sense they are in a position
of power such as by residing in a predominantly white environment
. . . they are more likely to identify with whites" (906). Of course,
Wilkinson doesn't say that the Latinos in these situations identify *as*
white, but it is not too difficult to extrapolate her position in regard
to my own relationship to whiteness via proximity.

However, my proximity to whiteness made me close to white
supremacy, too, a white supremacy that consistently molded my
identity.

THE PERSONALIZATION AND ASSIMILATION
OF WHITE SUPREMACY

I am not sure whether any of these factors listed above are explicitly
what made me choose to identify with and assimilate into whiteness and white supremacy, but I am certain my own proximity to
these social categories developed my identity. I saw the *power* of
whiteness all around me. It existed in the fabric of my hometown's
identity—how its residents fashioned themselves as a community—and their resistance to more diverse communities. To claim
Latinx identity in Grand Saline was to claim inferiority. I knew of
no Latinx leaders in the town. A few of my football coaches were

Latinx, but they situated themselves within whiteness and white supremacy by virtue of their appearance on the football field. They participated in the same racist charades as I did.

Overall, the stories of my first chapter illustrate both a white supremacist and an assimilationist rhetoric—showing how the language of assimilating into whiteness personally affected my identity.

The football story embodies these racist and assimilationist rhetorics. Moving to Grand Saline indoctrinated me into the community's racism from the very beginning. I didn't have to wait for my teenage peers to be explicit with the racism; I witnessed it from my coaches. Leading up to our games, the coaches would use the rhetoric of implicit racism to construct a white supremacist culture and ostracize Black students on the other teams. My coach teetered on the line of implicit racism by referring to the quarterback as faster than anything we have seen. Was their quarterback fast? Sure. But his playing ability was more about quick reactions and football intelligence, not based upon speed. These comments about speed are based upon a pseudoscientific, racist stance held by many people in the town: that Black people had extra leg muscles that made them faster. There are many myths about Black people and extra muscles in this country (Villarosa; Nunez-Smith et al.), and many times white people argue that such comments are jokes. That wasn't how it was presented in Grand Saline. It was a statement of fact. Rhetorically what makes stories like this so effective are not just the narratives themselves, but also the messengers. Our head coach, our father figure and the person we most respected because football was god, told us that Black people had extra muscles in their legs and were faster. His message, further developed via his ethos, told us that these types of narratives, based upon no science, should be accepted as truth. This is how implicit racism thrives in Grand Saline—elders in the community sell racist claims as "truth" to younger generations, who then repeat and recirculate these claims too (Sanchez, "Recirculating").

However, the story about one football game also shows a different type of rhetoric too, one of (anti-)assimilation. My friends in Grand Saline undoubtedly loved me. We were just as close as any friends could be. I would spend the night at their houses, we would go camping together, we did everything together. I never felt on the outside of my friendships. Yet even with this love, which was real, I was still on the *outside* of the white racial group. On the football field, I could be a co-leader and a great teammate, but I still wasn't white. When we were stretching and trying to intimidate the other team, one of my friends used explicit, anti-Black racism as a means to rhetorically create a whites-versus-Blacks divide. If he could turn this game into being not just about rival schools but rival races, then it could be a cry for our team to rally around. This was a rhetorical phenomenon found throughout the sports in Grand Saline—making them about race. One of the team's slogans my first couple of years of high school was "We're all right cuz we're all white!" That phrase, too, not only claims racial superiority (to be white is to be good or "all right") but also collectivizes the white majority, suggesting that when they work together as a race they can accomplish anything (which makes sense as a football slogan).

In this case, my friends understood that I wasn't a part of the white collective; I was outside of it. After the explicit racism was expressed, one of my friends was concerned for me. He acknowledged the hideous nature of the racism and wanted to shield me, a Brown person and his friend, from it. Some cognitive dissonance must have taken place here for this person to be fine with the explicit racism toward a Black person but want to protect me as a non-Black "other." Yet he was cognizant of my feelings, my outsider-ness, wanting me to still be a part of the group. I could be his great friend—maybe his best friend—but I still wasn't white.

The other friend acknowledged as much, saying that being Brown wasn't the same as being Black, which subscribes to a racial hierarchy, one described in the United States as white Americans at the top, African Americans (and sometimes Native Americans) at the bottom, and Asian Americans and Latinx peoples in the middle (Song 861). The racial hierarchy focuses on this white-versus-Black system and those in the middle can be closer to white or Black dependent upon different historical, societal, and political contexts (Omi and Winant; Walter). To both of my teammates, I was the same as them (same school, same football love, same team) until I wasn't (race and ethnicity). I could be partly white, or an honorary white, but there were still differences that could never be overcome, and I could be less than them at any moment.

Worse still is the fact that in that moment it was understood that I would side with their racism and their whiteness. I had nowhere else to go. This insider/outsider conversation forced me to join the whites on the same side of racism because I was on the same team as they were. If I *really* wanted to be one of them, I should join in the racism, without question. Even then, they'd make sure I knew my place.

I would always be beneath them on the racial hierarchy.

What happened to me in Grand Saline was a different sort of assimilationist rhetoric from that used with white people—one that invited me in sometimes (since I was different from my Black counterparts) and one that often made me still feel not "white" enough. This is because race is a binary system for people in the town, and Brown people could be moved between whiteness and otherness (not necessarily "Blackness") at a moment's notice because Brownness didn't have a well-defined meaning for the community. Racism was a problem for white and Black people, and the people in town viewed race from what Juan Perea calls a "Black/White binary paradigm," meaning that most white people viewed racism as solely being about white people versus Black people (Perea; Alcoff). Therefore, racism could never be done unto me from the white perspective because many white communities formulate race as the top of the hierarchy versus the bottom. This paradigm is a rhetorical construction as well, one whereby white people can situate Brown bodies as being for/against white people at any moment. The same can be said for other non-Black racialized bodies. In her study on Indigenous women's racialization at a university, for instance, Angelina E. Castagno found that "Indigenous women are constructed as Racialized Others among White peers and faculty and as White Others among non-Native peers of color. Either way, they are marginalized, objectified, and essentialized as something to be gazed *upon* rather than seen, heard, felt, and interacted *with*" (463). This corresponds with other research about non-Black minorities and how they exist in and outside of groups—or are simultaneously seen and not seen (Brayboy; Williams; Chang).

Nonetheless, with my dating story, it should be noted that my race and ethnicity still allowed me to sit at the table for dinner.

Many white people (and even some Latinx people) in Grand Saline are forbidden to date Black people. Though there were no Black people in town when I lived there, this ban on dating Black adolescents from other communities was embedded in many homes. Actually, during a shoot for *Man on Fire*, I received a message from a young white woman who had recently been kicked out of her house because she gave birth to a mixed-raced child with a young Black man. Though not every family in town abided by these rules, no doubt many—if not most—had similar bans.

However, on the particular occasion described in my story, I was able to enter this white home and eat dinner with this white family, even though I am not "white." I sat down at the table and enjoyed the spaghetti and dessert. I got to be there. That's more than might have been possible for most Black people trying to join family dinners in Grand Saline. Still, at the table, I didn't get the same privileges my white counterparts would have received. Mark, the dad, wasn't going to ask any white kids if their families had emigrated legally from Germany or Norway or some shit. Only the darker, nonwhite skin tones mattered in terms of legality.

Mark simultaneously allowed a Brown kid to feel welcomed into his home for dinner while making sure I didn't *completely* feel as though I belonged there. This odd version of assimilation—in being white enough to get to the table but still being questioned about whether I belonged there—encompasses my entire experience in the town. I moved in and out of groups whenever was convenient for the people at hand. So I could be white when we were facing Black people in a sports game or when wondering what races white girls in the town could date. But I also wasn't white because racism affected me and people wondered where my family "came" from.

My date's dad wanted me to be sure of that—even if he did so unintentionally.

For Brown people, many of our homes in the United States are never truly *home*. It doesn't matter where you live—Texas, California, Vermont—people still view you as a foreigner in your current space and place (Portes and Rumbaut). However, my date's dad used the innocuous, color-blind racist approach in discussing home with me. Though I didn't question him at the time and don't want to motivize[1] too much, I can't help parsing his logic. My race was open for discussion and potentially debate for him. Again, assuming that he wouldn't have asked a different white person in his house if their family had emigrated from some European country, he looked at my body and saw a topic of conversation, saw something that he, a white man, felt comfortable chatting about. His language focused on this othering of me. "Where are you from?" is a question that has been analyzed by many scholars of race in one form or another (Martinez, "Alejandra"). I think about how this question focuses on me being different but also in-between. My home must be different from the white people's—his question implies—but it also gives a space for some sort of acceptance, acceptance that didn't exist for the Black community. This is not to be an apologist for these remarks or to normalize them by any means, but rather to show the liminal space for Brown bodies in my community due to racial hierarchies and binary thinking. White people not only decided where certain people were on the hierarchy, but they also rhetorically situated them in these everyday encounters.

These encounters often intertwined race and ethnicity with socioeconomic status too.

When I was at the counselor's office planning for college, the counselor mistook my wanting to discuss higher education as a conversation about working after high school. It is impossible to know what factors led her to think this—potentially my ethnicity, the fact that I didn't come from any financial means, or maybe a mixture of both. Her attitude toward me illustrated some problem that existed between my grades and my personhood.

Assimilation asks outsiders to become insiders. Yet even when you assimilate into institutional norms—like being one of the top students in your graduating class even with a slacker's attitude—

that doesn't ever mean that the gatekeepers won't decide where you actually fit. How many "slackers" don't actually find their passion or intellectual chops until they reach the freedoms of college? Through all the debates on assimilation versus nationalism, debates where scholars often suggest that individual racialized people get a say in the matter, the truth is we don't. Or even when we do, the choices are arbitrary. I can decide that maybe I fit in better with white people than with Brown people, but that doesn't mean that white people view me the same way. The school counselor might see me as a good student—as good as anyone else—but she also might look at me and decide I don't truly fit into the higher education system. I must be preparing to enter the workforce, not college.

In our encounter, she first asked me if I was thinking of college, confused by why I would be in her presence during a time when all of my peers were planning for it. Her question inherently places me as an outsider. Why would *I* be thinking about college? She has the agency and rhetorical power in this moment to place me as an insider or an outsider. Had the counselor approached me with excitement or enthusiasm, ready to help me think about the next steps of my education, I might have felt like one of the group. However, she approached me with the opposite attitude; she treated me as if I didn't belong in her presence and as if the idea of college were too far-fetched for me. Even if it was not intentional, she forced me to the outside of the college bubble.

Even as someone who was often in this liminal in-between space where I could be made an insider or an outsider at a moment's notice, I gatekept too. In some sense, being someone in the in-between made me want to be a gatekeeper, so I could assimilate into the in-group. This is exactly what occurred when my friends and I made fun of Pablo for not speaking English. Though I did not want to laugh at him, and in hindsight wish I had stood up for him, I didn't, because it provided me some agency in assimilating into my white friend group. If I hadn't joined in the bullying, I would have maintained my outsider status. This was a way for me to prove my worth, and I fell for the peer pressure—just as all of those 1990s DARE public-service announcement videos told me not to do.

Assimilation is tricky. Even when my language practices (bullying in this instance) demonstrated some insider knowledge and acceptance, it still did not provide me full access to whiteness. I could prove my worth and try my hardest to fit in, but at the end of the day, the choice wasn't mine. My race and ethnicity, my Brownness and Chicanx nature, made me a perpetual outsider in the in-between space—one who could be the teammate on the football field but still not be white, could sit at the table and eat with the white family but still be questioned about my heritage, could have the grades of anyone else in my class but still be asked whether college was for me, could befriend someone who didn't speak much English but could still make fun of them in order to fit into whiteness. My entire high school experience revolved around my liminal state of assimilation.

THE INSTITUTIONALIZATION OF WHITE SUPREMACY

My personal stories illustrate how white supremacy and assimilation affected my life, but these stories would never have been shared if racism hadn't been institutionalized in Grand Saline, and though I didn't explicitly talk about the systemic racism in my stories, it is ever-present. It thrives in the football program, one of most well-established institutions in the school and in Grand Saline as a whole. These interrelated institutions create an atmosphere for white supremacy to flourish and to be tolerated, where no one ever questions it, and they are the reason the culture of racism in Grand Saline has remained intact for decades (if not over a century). It is a legacy passed down from generation to generation, indoctrinating anyone who steps into a school hallway in Grand Saline or puts on the pads and helmet to play football for the school.

In the town's football culture, white supremacy wasn't even an implicit practice; it was overt. As I discuss in *Race, Rhetoric, and Research Methods* (Lockett et al.), the locker room was the most toxic environment I had ever seen. Teammates, including me, consistently made racist, sexist, and other bigoted comments before and after practices and on the football field itself. Anything cruel and demeaning was fair game in this atmosphere because no one was held responsible for anything they said. Often, the crueler comments carried the most weight. Saying the most outlandish, terrible, bigoted things was a point of pride in the locker-room space. I remember discussing who was or was not promiscuous in our high school (using overtly sexist language), calling anyone and everyone homophobic slurs, and being surrounded by racism. People generally understand the toxicity of these spaces, as when Donald Trump made headlines in 2016 for talking about sexually assaulting women and it was dubbed "locker-room talk" (Fahrenthold). For some reason, dubbing something "locker-room talk"—or implying that such prejudiced talk is okay when men are talking in private to other men—was meant to suggest that what Trump said was okay. Such behavior is allowed in locker rooms. I wholeheartedly disagree, though the same logic applies to the locker room in Grand Saline. The worst things I have ever heard anyone say occurred in that space.

However, what makes this "talk" so terrible and systemic isn't just that anyone could say anything, it was that coaches often took part in this practice as well, establishing that we *should* join in this bigoted practice. Coaches claimed that Black students had extra muscles in their legs, told us not to make Black rivals mad because they become better athletes when they are upset, and stayed silent when students participated in racism. They reinforced white supremacy through their active promotion of racial slurs, "jokes," and racist myths and through their failure to correct students who repeated discriminatory language. Many of the coaches participated in the racist jokes, and never, in my entire middle school and high school experiences, did they ever challenge such biases. They created spaces for students to believe that bigotry wasn't only tolerated but was openly acceptable. White supremacy created community and identity because race was often the butt of jokes and was something that Grand Saline could bond around as one of the only schools without Black students in the division.

Nothing suggests that my years playing football in Grand Saline were unique in the history of the town and the football program. Why would Grand Saline only be more bigoted when I was there?

When I was a first-year student in high school, I heard the varsity football team's slogan, "We're all right cuz we're all white!" I doubt that was a slogan that was created the year I started high school. Actually, it would seem more likely that when Grand Saline was less diverse, the football team might have been even more aligned with explicit white supremacy. However, the institutional nature of this white supremacy occurs because racism—like Grand Saline's storied football program—is a tradition in the high school locker room. It is taught by upperclassmen as a rite of passage for underclassmen, established as what the locker room should be about. Coaches reinforce white supremacy even more effectively than older students because their jokes, comments, and/or silence show what is acceptable and tolerated in this space. To play football in Grand Saline is to be indoctrinated into white supremacy, feeling the full brunt of bigotry and racist ideologies. But white supremacy didn't flourish only in the locker room; it was acceptable in the entire school experience as well.

The slogan "We're all right cuz we're all white!" was not just said in front of teammates and coaches; it was actually a slogan heard at the end of pep rallies in the gym (I don't think we used the slogan during all of my time in high school, but I know we did my first couple of years). We repeated this phrase in front of other students, teachers, family members, and elders in the community. Of course, I am certain not all of them could hear it, but I have no doubt that many of them did. This haunts me now because I can see their faces cheering us on from the gymnasium stands. Some of the teachers I love, some of them I hate. Coaches I admire and aspire to be. Parents of some of my best friends. I watch the smiles on their faces as they cheer on the team before our game and the excitement and energy they bring to that space. Unfortunately, those smiles don't dissipate after we yell our team slogan. They are still smiling.

Sam Adams, a late-twenties white woman who went to Grand Saline High School, talked to me about her high school experience: "Racism was very apparent in all of high school. . . . I often got called [racist names] for dating a Black boy, and I heard racial epithets in high school every day." She's not the only one to believe that the high school had a systemic racism problem. Emily Erwin, a mid-thirties white woman, remembers being in high school and acting "ghetto" (or Black) as a part of a pep rally and claims that this memory haunts her because none of the teachers or elders in the room ever thought to say how "acting Black" was wrong. These are just a couple of instances of people remembering the pain of systemic racism in the high school, but they highlight the problem that no one ever spoke up against white supremacy in the school.

As in the locker room, complicity was also often front and center elsewhere in high school. Derogatory, racist comments could be made in front of fellow students—even students of color—and most people wouldn't do anything. I can't even remember a single discussion revolving around white supremacy or racism as a problem, not from teachers, students, or anyone. Discussing racism was a nonstarter. The climate in the high school was that white supremacy was tolerated, some of it explicit, but especially the implicit versions. I don't ever remember a teacher joining in on this discourse, but they were definitely silent in the face of it. They had to hear it. I can't imagine a teacher existing in that space for even a month without being fully aware of the high school's embrace of white supremacy. No one participated in nuanced discussions of race or racism, even when the town is known as one of the most racist places in the state of Texas. I don't want to judge these teachers too harshly; obviously there are constraints in what they can teach. But I can't help thinking about how just one teacher who practiced antiracism could have made a difference in this space.

The school was also complicit in its silence because all of the teachers, administrators, and others heard white supremacy in one shape or another and did nothing. Institutionally, this told students that racism was an acceptable mode of discourse in the high school, and the people who spread this hate in the locker room also spread it in the high school as a whole. With the various stories about the history of racism in the town (examined in Chapter 3 and 4), the regular use of racial epithets and other bigoted sentiments in classrooms, in the hallways, and in the high school social life, white supremacy became cultural knowledge for anyone who entered school grounds.

However, these aren't the only systemic acts of racism that occur in Grand Saline, though these are the structures that often affect kids and teenagers the most. The Grand Saline Public Housing Authority was sued in 1985—in part of the largest desegregation lawsuit in the history of public housing—by the United States (Loewen; Hartman and Squires). The class-action lawsuit was brought against multiple Housing and Urban Development (HUD)–assisted housing projects in East Texas because these towns had not integrated Black people into their public housing. In the summary statement from the lawsuit—*Young v. Pierce* (1985)—the court found that "the vast majority of [housing] projects are predominantly one race. . . . (3) Blacks participate disproportionally in older insured-assisted projects; (4) whites participate disproportionately in Section 8 new construction projects; and (5) the races have roughly equivalent needs for public housing." The court found that the plaintiffs demonstrated that they were victims of discrimination and segregation and ruled in their favor. In the appendix of the suit, the court provided the breakdowns of public housing for all thirty-six counties mentioned in the lawsuit. Grand Saline—along with Van—were the two towns with no Black people in their public housing. The town systemically didn't allow Black people into their lower-income apartments.

However, as the landmark *Brown v. Board of Education* case demonstrated, the enforcement of desegregation after a lawsuit doesn't come easy. Grand Saline failed for years to get Black people into their public housing, probably for multiple reasons, including the town's reputation (Stewart). Nevertheless, in the mid-1990s, a Black family moved into the public housing—the Robinsons. People I interviewed echoed many different rumors about the Robinson family. "They had the police always watching over them" (Amanda Jones, an early-thirties white Grand Saline native); "The FBI had to protect them" (Adams); "They were eventually run out of town" (Sasha Mann). Many people heard rumors (none of which could be proven) about the family, but all the rumors suggested that the family had to be protected and that the family departed from the town quickly after moving there. Local historian Elvis

Allen combats this story, saying that nothing bad ever happened with the family. I eventually interviewed Lincoln, one of the Robinson children, over fifteen years after he left the town. He didn't have anything bad to say about the community on the surface.[2] His descriptions and memories weren't completely positive or nostalgic, but he didn't have any ill-will toward Grand Saline. Nonetheless, the Robinsons didn't stay in Grand Saline for too long. The family was only in town for a few school years.

Eventually, the Robinsons left, and there were no more Black people living in the public housing in the community. Many residents argue that Black people didn't want to move to town because they heard of the town's racism—or heard about the Robinson family's departure—and believed that it wasn't safe for them to live there. This thus becomes a rhetorical defense for the town: it's not that they don't want Black residents; Black residents don't want them. But Grand Saline's legacy as a sundown town and its previous segregation policies keep people from wanting to move into the community because the townsfolk didn't *actively* try to change anything. If this town has a bad reputation and doesn't attempt to change it, why would a Black family want to move to town? Arguably, this could be a bad consequence of the past, and maybe the town has changed over the decades but just doesn't know how to move forward. However, some might argue that this logic solely serves as a defense for the town to prevent more Black people from moving in. By not showing themselves as changed, the people of Grand Saline can be sure that no one new will want to be a part of their community.

Ultimately, this is how nothing changes in Grand Saline. Though elders in the community can claim that the town and its culture have no problem, my experiences (especially on the football team and in the high school), others' memories, and the public housing debacle demonstrate how white supremacy thrives. It exists in the taunting of basketball players of color who played in our gym. It thrives in the jokes and stories told among high schoolers. It presides over the lack of diversity in the public housing. Town members consistently repeat racist tropes and never speak out against them when they know they should, and that creates a space for white supremacy to be tolerable. That tolerance cannot change unless it is forced to, and if the people never leave this community and reside only in this bubble, they latch on to this mindset. They constitute a community of white supremacy.

In Grand Saline, racism exists in a few different forms—in the systemic structures of the housing authority, the high school, and the football program and via a distorted assimilationist rhetoric, where I, as a Chicanx, could move around and be both victim of and participant in racism at any time. My stories and this research illustrate the versatility of such models for mixed-raced or Brown people and how they can adapt at any time. I could be white when needed—when playing against Black people in football or when making fun of the student who couldn't speak English well—but I could also be Brown and different too—when being asked about my heritage or when talking about college. Ultimately, I had some agency in these situations with aligning myself with certain races and even white supremacy at times, but the decision wasn't always mine. The institutional white supremacy forced me into particular circumstances as well.

Most important, these stories and my analysis demonstrate that assimilation doesn't just apply to racial formations and identities but can devise racist ideologies too. I was taught to be a white supremacist if I wanted to be cool, if I wanted to fit into football culture, if I wanted to keep things smooth with my friends. In a culture where racism is capital, assimilating into bigotry is a necessity, especially for one's popularity to survive.

However, the stories I remember aren't just about personal racism and rhetorics of assimilation; they go much deeper. The stories I remember don't always involve me—they are the racist legends the town has told and has continued to circulate for decades or perhaps even over a century.

3

The Truth about Stories

THERE'S AN AXIOM IN public memory scholarship that has stuck with me since I began my research—what a society chooses to remember (via public memorials, statues, remembrance days, and more) shows you what that society deems important. We don't create memorials to people or ideas we don't care about, and this is clearly seen in studying the South and memories of the Confederacy. The history of how and why Confederate memorials were built isn't the issue at hand;[1] rather, it is important to note that these memorials still exist today, decades and sometimes over a century after they were created, because they still denote identity for some people in the South. They still sustain culture for many southerners.

For instance, Confederate Memorial Day is still celebrated in Alabama, Georgia, Texas, and other states. Millions of people trek to Stone Mountain, Georgia, each year to celebrate the bas-relief carvings of Jefferson Davis, Robert E. Lee, and Thomas "Stonewall" Jackson in the area rock, and it is the most visited tourist attraction in the state (Bell). The state of Mississippi had the battle flag of the Army of Northern Virginia—popularly known as representing the Confederacy—in their state flag until the state governor signed a bill to change it in 2020 (Berman and Guarino). The University of Mississippi has at least twenty monuments and buildings named after or dedicated to Confederate soldiers and generals. And while recent Black Lives Matter protests have ended with Confederate monuments being removed, or sometimes toppled, these memorials still stand and mark value across the South. These monuments and memorials exist not as means just to represent the past or history but to substantiate identity. Millions of people descend on these sites and wear shirts and hats depicting Confederate symbolism because it represents who they are—connecting these memories to their "heritage" of southernness. Many others, me included, disagree with this interpretation and see these commemorations as indicative of a heritage of hatred and oppression.

Most important, these symbols and monuments of the Confederacy exist in our present—over 150 years after the Civil War ended—because some people still *identify* with them, or, as Benedict Anderson would say, this is the way some southern communities imagine themselves. Some people tell these stories of the Confederacy to themselves and to their descendants to signify the importance of this memory and how it reflects their identity, even when millions of Americans associate these symbols with pain and terror. They tell stories about who they are and where they came from, and Confederate symbols reflect the values enshrined in these tales.

However, the southerners who imagine themselves as a part of this community aren't the only ones who fashion themselves via controversial storytelling traditions. In Grand Saline, three particular stories build identity for people in the town—stories about lynchings at Poletown, the KKK at Clark's Ferry, and Grand Saline's being a sundown town. These stories build and manifest white supremacist identity for residents and were as much of a part of the town's culture and heritage as anything else during my high school days.

POLETOWN

About two miles west of downtown Grand Saline lies Poletown. Poletown is the place where the "white trash" live, or so goes the talk in Grand Saline. In reality, Poletown remains one of the poorest neighborhoods in the area, comprising mostly trailers, unmowed lawns, and unpaved roads, but it is not much different from the rest of the town, honestly. Hence, "Po-town."

One distinct memory stands out for me here: the *thud, thud, thud* of tires rolling over the jagged Poletown Bridge. Grand Saline isn't too big a town, so there aren't many bridges in the area. Actually, it was the only wooden bridge I remember crossing around the area.

On weekend nights in high school, when my friends and I wanted to score some beer, we would head over the Poletown Bridge to the bootlegger, a middle-aged white man who lived in an old shack that was part trailer and part house and would sell teenagers beers by the dollar. This, undoubtedly, was a bad deal for lots of reasons (thirty dollars for thirty beers, especially when the beers were often Busch Lite or Keystone, doesn't make a lot of sense). In high school, I always associated this transaction with this space, connected it to being poor, and subjected it to the stereotypes of "Po-town." The old, run-down bridge we had to cross to enter the neighborhood (instead of taking the back roads that would make the trip a few minutes longer) was emblematic of the place.

The long-standing wooden planks that had formed the bridge decades earlier were doing their best to barely hold everything together in the early 2000s. Townsfolk had a running joke about who would be the driver who fell to their death when the bridge eventually collapsed. Back in high school, I was an evangelical Christian, and I distinctly remember saying little prayers each time we trekked over the bridge—hoping this wasn't the time the faithful planks finally caved in—and also praying that whatever I got into in that area I would still be safe. The *thuds* of the bridge reminded me that life is precarious but also that I had not fallen to my death quite yet. The *thuds* also helped me understand how I associate material artifacts with place.

Still, Poletown and the bridge don't represent only the impoverished, or shady high school dealings, for me—a much darker history lies beneath the planks, one that shows that the stories of racism in my hometown—while disturbing and insidious—often say more about the racism of the storyteller than any historical truth.

One night, when I was in my first year of high school, I was invited to Poletown to hang out at the rodeo grounds (just a stone's throw away from the bridge) and drink beer with some older students. This was one of my first experiences hanging out with kids from the grades above me, so I took it as a chance to prove my coolness.

Johnny, a junior, picked me up from my house near the train tracks and handed me a cheap beer (probably one from the bootlegger) as soon as I got into his truck. Johnny was a white, wide-shouldered student and a football teammate who played the same position as me. He had taken me under his wing a bit, as we had similar frames and play styles on the offensive line. I was just happy that someone older had liked me enough to break the law with me on a Saturday night.

"Chug that beer! We're going to the rodeo grounds to meet with some people!" he exclaimed.

I took a big sip of the beer, until the bitterness got the best of me, and we took off down the road. It was around eleven o'clock.

"How's practice been going lately?" he asked as we turned onto the major highway in town.

"Not bad. It's pretty easy when I'm practicing against the junior varsity, but with some of those bigger guys on the varsity, it's tough."

I took a few more swigs to try to keep pace with him. I couldn't let him think I was new to drinking (though I had been to maybe one or two parties before this). He turned off the music.

"Yeah, yeah. You'll get the hang of it eventually. . . . Hey, you're still pretty new here. Have you ever been out to the rodeo grounds or know the story of the Poletown Bridge?"

Since middle school, I had heard bits and pieces about the bridge but had never received a full version of the tale. I told Johnny I hadn't heard it.

He smiled and took a drink of his beer. He was happy to recount the legend.

"Well, back in the day, we used to lynch lots of n------ in Grand Saline." His smile never faded as we turned onto the Poletown Bridge road. "We would lynch them and hang their bodies over this bridge so the train could hit them. This was a warning for n------ on the train coming into town . . . to show they weren't welcome here."

Each of the bridge's planks welcomed us.

Thud, thud, thud.

"And then they would cut their heads from their bodies and put them on poles in the area as a warning for others who didn't travel by train. So that's where the name 'Poletown' comes from."

We pulled into the rodeo grounds where a few people had already gathered. He parked the car and turned off his headlights and looked to me. "Don't worry—we haven't done that in years."

His smile widened.

Johnny finished his beer and threw it on the ground outside the car on his way out. I followed closely behind. I had only finished half of my beer, so I made sure to pour the rest of it out because I didn't want him to hear the sounds of a half full beer can hitting the ground. I had to stay a part of the group.

Ten of us sat in the rodeo grounds that night and drank ourselves into oblivion, or most of them did while I struggled to finish the alcohol provided. Still, I couldn't help looking back toward the bridge—thinking about the past, thinking about the lives lost all around us. But here we were, mostly white kids and me, drinking near this haunting ground as if the dead don't speak to us.

A few hours later, when I stupidly let Johnny drive me home after he had guzzled a few more beers, I felt a specific fear as we arrived at the bridge—something I didn't understand at the time—so I closed my eyes as we crossed it. In hindsight, I think I was trying to hide from the horrors that my friend had so cheerfully expressed to me.

During the rest of my time in high school, I heard the same story, but I often pushed it to the back of my mind when I took the bridge as a shortcut to purchase beer or travel to some friends' houses. After I left Grand Saline, I only traveled back to this spot twice—once while filming local historian Elvis Allen in the summer of 2016 as he discussed the history of lynching for *Man on Fire* and once over winter break in December 2019 with my partner and my mom.

By 2016 the bridge had long been torn down without something else to replace it. The edges of the road leading up to the spot where the bridge once stood were overrun with tall grass, obscuring our view of the train tracks. During filming, Allen recounted a story of a white doctor whose head was placed on a pole because he treated Black people in the area. (He had previously denied that Poletown had any racist connotations.) Yet I could still feel the bridge's presence hovering over me in that moment—its shadow looming with the stories of decades prior. Throughout the interview, while trying to pay full attention to Allen, I kept looking back toward the space where the bridge once was, remembering all the times I crossed it over the years. I was glad to see it gone.

In December 2019, I returned to Grand Saline after living in Vermont for a few years. I wanted my mom and girlfriend to visit the parking lot where Charles Moore self-immolated. I also needed to pay homage to his life and death because I hadn't been in town since creating the documentary. I owed much of my scholarship and career to Moore's sacrifice and wanted to reflect on the past five years of work. After spending a few moments in the lot, we headed toward the torn-down bridge for more reflection. While driving there, I noticed how little had changed, except for a new gas station resting on the west side of town.

As I turned onto the Poletown Bridge road, a rebuilt, paved bridge welcomed us. I expressed my shock that someone had finally decided to replace it. Being back in that spot—and seeing a new bridge—overwhelmed me with an innate desire to take in the memory of the *thud*.

Our tires spun over the smooth asphalt without a peep.

The *thud, thud, thud* had disappeared with the old wooden planks.

I assume the memory of the old bridge followed suit.

CLARK'S FERRY

Whereas Poletown tells the story of lynchings of Black people, Clark's Ferry focuses on a different racialized legend, one of the Ku Klux Klan.

About seven miles north of town—down some rocky roads and unkempt paths—lies Clark's Ferry, on the edge of the Sabine River. The space itself is inconspicuous enough. It consists of a dirt turnaround by the riverbed, surrounded by a deep, dark wood, and has been a hotspot for backroading—what southerners and Texans call drinking and driving on empty roads in rural spaces—for years. Many high schoolers voyaged to this site on the weekends, putting miles between them and their parents and guardians.

However, the legend of Clark's Ferry (less specific than Pole-town) reveals that this was a popular meeting spot for the KKK in the latter parts of the twentieth century and maybe even when I was in high school during the early 2000s. This is where the Klan would hold bonfires and rallies. There's enough anecdotal evidence to believe this could be true. One man, Chance Sauseda, told the *Houston Chronicle* in the 1990s that he had traveled to Clark's Ferry one evening and saw a Klan rally taking place. He stated he left the area as quickly as possible in fear of what would have happened if he had been caught (Stewart). Other people state that they have seen the Klan operating at Clark's Ferry and in town (Fite; "36 Texas Counties"), and that there is just a general fear of the Klan in this space (according to Billy Knope, a white man who graduated with me, and Diana Wilt, a late-twenties white woman). The story of the Klan at Clark's Ferry is less about actualized racial terror—as it is at the Poletown Bridge—and more about representative and symbolic racial crimes.

Then there was the time I partook in a "prank" near Clark's Ferry with both racist and sexist overtones.

Toward the end of my sophomore year of high school, I was close friends with some seniors who wanted to pull off a senior prank that town members would discuss for decades, basing it on the lore of Clark's Ferry. Eight senior boys, and I and another sophomore, Marcus, one of my best friends, would lay a trap to scare some of the senior girls. Eight of us would go out to a pasture near Clark's Ferry, dressed all in black, and act as if we were a part of the occult by building a fire and reciting fake chants. Then two of the senior boys would trick six of our female friends to ride out to Clark's Ferry with them, and we would jump out of the woods and scare them. The story would, we hoped, be legend for years to come.

The Saturday night before graduation, one of my senior friends came to my house and picked up me and Marcus. We were dressed mostly in black and ready for the ruse.

"Chase, why are you wearing jeans?" the senior shouted as Marcus and I walked toward his truck. "You're supposed to be all in black!"

"I don't have black jeans, man," I retorted. "And it'll be dark anyway. They won't be able to tell!"

We drove to the old turnaround in the woods as the sunset light filtered through the trees and parked our cars further up the road.

Then we waited . . . for what seemed like hours.

This was in the early age of cell phones—when you had to pay for each text you sent—so we weren't in constant update with our two friends who were attempting to lure the senior girls into the prank. We stood in an open field at the edge of the road building a fire, dressed in our dark garb, waiting to scare these young women.

But something kept gnawing away at me as we prepared our stunt: Was this, actually, the same spot where the KKK held bonfires and rallies? If we changed the color of attire from black to white, I most certainly wouldn't be welcomed here. Does the KKK still meet out here? What if some of them are on the edge of the woods now, waiting for us?

I spooked myself and stepped away from the fire-building to gather my composure.

"Is something wrong?" a voice called from behind me. It was Bryan, one of the seniors who had helped organized the stunt.

"Yeah, I'm fine." I looked up. He was dressed all in black, and the light from the newly formed fire covered half of his face. The night held the other half.

I walked back to the fire with the certainty that we didn't belong here—or more specifically that I, the only nonwhite person doing the prank, didn't belong here. To keep calm, I kept adding twigs and branches to the flame.

Eventually we received the text that our friends were on the way there with the girls, and that the girls were even the ones who suggested they check out Clark's Ferry!

Most of the guys gathered around the fire to begin fake chanting while Marcus and I scampered further down the road to throw smoke bombs. The truck would have to drive by and see this fire before turning around at the end of the road, where Marcus and I would heave bombs at them to add intensity and mystique to the scene. We waited in some bushes at the end of the turnaround in the complete darkness. I don't remember exactly what we talked about, but I remember being so nervous about the prank and afraid of the space we were in that I kept making nervous small talk.

Finally we saw headlights edge over the top of the hill and got into position to throw our smoke bombs. The truck stopped by the fire, the chants commenced, the girls screamed, and the truck sped toward us. We were successful in the first act. The screams continued as the truck reached the turnaround and our smoke bombs littered the area with a lingering haze.

"What is going on!?!" I could hear one of the girls yell as the vehicle quickly U-turned back toward the fire. By now, the boys had placed a big log—also on fire—in front of the road, blocking the truck from exiting. The vehicle stopped in front of the log and the two senior boys got out and started play-fighting with the group (how could this even look believable?). After seemingly minutes—but actually only a few seconds—one of the girls jumped in the front seat and rammed the truck over the log. The guys quickly scrambled back into the car (afraid of the damage to the wheels) and took off down the road. We de-masked and congratulated ourselves on the best prank we thought we could ever pull. The girls had been terrorized and secretly I had been terrorized too.

Marcus was dating one of the senior girls, so we rushed back to my place (my mom was away for the weekend) to act as if we weren't part of the prank. His girlfriend called him, hectically recounting her story, as we changed into our normal clothes and destroyed all evidence that we had been in on the scare. Eventually, she and another senior girl came over and told us what happened from my living-room couch.

It was immediately apparent that we had caused too much harm—these young women truly felt that they had been attacked by the occult. That wasn't their only theory of what occurred.

"You know," my friend's girlfriend said after calming down a bit, "that *is* where the KKK meets. . . . What if that was the KKK?"

I responded quickly: "Yeah, but you said these guys were wearing dark clothes and dark masks. Doesn't the KKK wear all white?" I was clearly being defensive, but they couldn't tell in that moment.

"Maybe . . . Maybe they were dressed differently. Who knows?"

I never imagined the terror I caused could be mistaken for the actions of the KKK (understanding that the true terror the KKK causes is objectively worse), but it reminds me of how much place and symbolism can be tied together. Just the perception of our nefarious activities made these girls connect us to the history of the Klan in that area.

I was now a part of another story that people would tell about that space.

I am a part of the story of Clark's Ferry.

A week later, the girls found out about the prank and were upset with us for a few days, but they got over it fairly promptly.

Soon after I graduated from high school, the owner of the property that included Clark's Ferry placed a fence and gate on the estate, with a sign stating that trespassers would be prosecuted. He was tired of high schoolers treating his land as their own personal playground.

I talked with a few kids who recently graduated from the high school, and they had heard bits and pieces of the story, but it doesn't hold the same weight in the cultural imaginary as it did when I was in school there. Nonetheless, the story—even if not fully formed—persists.

THE SUNDOWN-TOWN SIGNS

While these two stories of racism and racial terror are built around particular places, the final story of Grand Saline being a "sundown town" is quite a bit different. "Sundown towns" are communities that forbid African Americans from living within their city limits. James W. Loewen notes that they were so named "because many marked their city limits with signs typically reading, 'N-----, Don't Let The Sun Go Down on You In ___'" (1). Loewen confirms Grand Saline as a sundown town in his Sundown Towns in the United States, a site dedicated to the curation of sundown-town histories. One oral history in Loewen's entry on Grand Saline claims that the residents purged their town of Black people after the Reconstruction era, "killing all who were unable to escape. . . . [T]he mass killings were followed by mutilation of the corpses for public display." A former slave who traveled through town even said that "[they] had a big sign [there with] 'N-----, don't let [the] sun go down on you here' on it." Grand Saline's sundown-town status seems well-recorded through oral history—through these accounts in Loewen's research and the storytelling of the town—yet the actual place of the sign(s) remains unknown in these stories. I associate them with these two, large welcoming signs on each side of Highway 80.

Highway 80, the only major road in town, runs parallel to the train tracks and is the main entrance from the east and the west. On both sides of town along Highway 80 are signs welcoming guests into the community. From the east, the sign reads "Welcome to Grand Saline" with the town's nickname, "Salt of the Earth," beneath it (see Figure 3). Once probably a shining beacon of warmth and community, the sign is now decaying, peeling from the wood on which it rests.

Figure 3. The welcome sign from the east.

Figure 4. The sign from the west entrance.

From the west stands a newer, smaller sign greeting visitors (Figure 4). The sign reads, "Welcome," above an image of the state of Texas (displayed in red, white, and blue). A saltshaker is painted in the middle of the sign, pouring salt onto West Texas. Beneath the sign is, again, the town's nickname, "Salt of The [sic] Earth."

When I close my eyes, I think back to what Grand Saline looked like in the pre–Civil Rights era when these signs existed. What would it have looked like to be passing through town on the way to Dallas or going toward Louisiana and seeing signs—signs that existed maybe where the entrance signs are now—telling Black people they weren't welcome here? I never had physical encounters with these signs because no one in town knows where they were exactly (or at least the younger people don't), and I know most people I have interviewed about these stories, especially older folk, tell me that the signs are just folklore and the stories about them are unfounded.

Many times, people would tell these stories of Grand Saline's sundown status as "jokes"—"jokes" they would dismiss as just being "humorous" but which often illuminate some racist ideology.

While filming *Man on Fire*, I interviewed a bunch of older men in the local coffee shop about these stories, focusing intently on the story of the sundown town signs. Our film crew arrived at a refurbished pharmacy—now touted as a coffee shop and "museum" of the town—ready to film in June 2016. I felt nervous entering this space because I didn't really know any of these older men, and, as the interviewer for the film, didn't know how they'd react to the questions I wanted to ask.

The man who invited us took us around the museum where they had old pictures of the town and other oddities, including a hat rack for local men who have died to hang their cowboy hats "six feet up on the wall because they're six feet under the ground," before introducing us to four older white men playing dominoes.

We shook hands with the men, who were all sitting around the table. I could tell that they preferred us not to be in their space, but none of them objected to our presence or the film contracts we asked them to sign before shooting.

"These are the hardworking men of Grand Saline," our host proclaimed. "Without them the town would just fold."

All of us laughed, and the film crew began setting up our equipment for the film shoot. The tension eased a bit.

A few minutes later, one of them said loudly: "Chase Sanchez, huh?" I was setting up the lights.

"Yes, sir?"

"Did you play football here in the early 2000s? I remember you.
. . ."

I was shocked that anyone would remember me, or our mediocre high school football team, over a decade later, but that's Texas. Football surpasses everything else. I figured that someone remembering me could help me position myself as an "insider." I was still, partly, one of them.

We reminisced about the old football traditions as the rest of the team finished setting up the equipment. (One of my primary goals as the interviewer was to make the interviewees as comfortable as possible before we began shooting.)

The cameras began rolling and we watched the men play their game of dominoes while asking them questions about why they love the town—the softball questions before getting to the tougher ones on Charles Moore and the town's racist history. It took me awhile to build up the courage to ask some of them.

"So," I nervously fumbled into one question, "what about the stories of Grand Saline being a sundown town? I remember hearing about them when I was here. What do y'all think about them?" I tried to give the question more gravitas by acknowledging that I remembered the stories too.

"They're just old wives' tales," one man chirped. "These are just stories boys would tell to scare other boys or girls and stuff."

The other men nodded in agreement.

"You know," one of them began after a few seconds of silence, "we would always tell this story about these signs and this sheriff that used to live in town in the fifties and sixties. If he caught a Black man in town, especially after dark, he'd get him and take him to the outskirts of town and bury him up to his head. And then the sheriff would spit on him and scare him so much that when he eventually unburied him, he knew that the Black man would never come back to town again."

He started laughing. No one else did.

"I remember hearing it and telling that story for years!" his laugh faded as he studied the dominoes in front of him.

At first, I assumed this was being told as simply another "old wives' tale," but by the end of it, I was unsure. He sounded as if he believed it.

Eventually we finished filming for the day and left Grand Saline with a fruitful shoot, but this story weighed on Joel and me. What was the truth? "I think he really thinks it's true," I told Joel on the way back to the house we were staying in. "Even if he laughed it off, as you would a joke, he meant it. I mean, it still sounds outlandish. It would take a lot of effort to bury someone and then dig them up." Joel agreed but asked me how I could tell that the domino player thought the story was true. I didn't have a great answer. "It's just, like, the comfort he had in telling that story. You wouldn't tell that to outsiders if you didn't think it was true."

We ventured back into town, about a month later, and stopped by the coffee shop again because we had two historians in the area we wanted to interview in this setting. It captured the right mood.

Right when we arrived, the old man who told us the sheriff story walked over to us with something on his mind.

"I want to apologize," he began. I could tell from his voice and his face that he felt as though he had made a mistake. He sounded sincere.

"After y'all left a few weeks back, all the other guys got mad at me. 'Why did you tell them that story!' they told me. I shouldn't have told you that. It was all . . . it was all just a joke. Just, would you all mind deleting that? I don't want that in the film."

There's a whole ethical gray area of using interview footage that someone has legally signed off on in a film if they ask you not to use it (we ultimately decided it didn't fit the narrative we wanted to create), but, more important, I was shocked by this man's response, which was representative of the racism and racist folklore in Grand Saline.

He wasn't upset that he had told a "joke" (even though I thought he believed it and was only saving face afterwards) that supported the existence of racial subjugation in Grand Saline. He was upset that his friends thought he made them look bad or that he might appear racist in the film. He wanted us to protect his image or the image of the town; he didn't see how his actions circulated racism. This is a truth about individual prejudice and racism for most people—they don't care that they are racist; they just don't want to be *perceived* as racist.

Ultimately, that's what I remember most about these stories in Grand Saline. It doesn't matter whether the stories of the lynchings, or the KKK, or the sundown town are true or not—from a racial lens—because the fact that the stories are all told over and over and over as "jokes" or "history" (also not as warnings) expresses more information than if they were objectively true.

Why tell these racist stories in the first place? Why create a community where almost everyone—if not everyone—in the town knows these stories and can repeat them? Why joke about racial murder and violence at all?

These are the questions I have now, as a scholar interested in memory, race, and rhetoric, but back when I was a kid in town, I didn't ask these questions. I heard these stories and told them as everyone else did. I laughed at them. I didn't know whether they could truly affect anyone, but that didn't really matter to me.

It matters to me now.

4

Where There's Smoke

The truth about stories is that's all we are.
—Thomas King, *The Truth about Stories*

WE ALL HAVE STORIES WE tell ourselves and others about who we are.

I have stories I tell myself about perseverance (*Remember that time your old college advisor doubted you?*), about kindness (*Remember that time your grandfather taught you you should always give to people in need, even if you doubt their motives?*), about familial love (*Remember that time your mother rode with you cross-country to move you to Vermont?*), and about bootstrap myths (*Remember being the only researcher from an R2 school during your orientation at Middlebury College?*). I often reflect on these memories in times of anxiety or uncertainty, when I need something to center me after feeling lost or not myself for a while.

I tell myself stories to remind myself who I am and what I believe.

In this solitary tradition, my personal stories hold tremendous power. They are able to take me from a state of depression or anxiety or anger and move me back to something that feels more like my "normal" self. These stories become the centerpiece for who I think I am, and even though I mostly only tell these stories inside my own head, they often become stories I tell others, hoping that I might help fashion myself and my family to them in a similar light.

But what happens when the stories we tell about ourselves—the stories we tell one another, as a part of a group, and to others outside of our community—fashion us differently, in a more negative light? How does that affect how we view ourselves and how we view others? How do outsiders view us when they hear these stories?

In Grand Saline, storytelling has a specific rhetorical power—
it delineates culture and white supremacist ideology, even if only
implicitly. The stories in the previous chapter show me coming to
understand the power of stories in specific ways—be it the violence
embedded within the site of a bridge, a memory of the Klan, or
the ways people mask hatred within "jokes." These "jokes" helped
me understand who I was in relation to the rest of the community,
what the community believes to be true, how they represent their
ideologies, and how outsiders perceive Grand Saline. Storytelling is
unique in Grand Saline because though every community has stories about themselves, the racist stories of my hometown are known
to people all across the state of Texas. Michael Hall, an author for
Texas Monthly who wrote a long-read article on Charles Moore,
told me he has talked to people across the state about Grand Saline,
and believes it is known as either "the most or second most racist area in the state, behind the Jasper and Vidor region," where a
lynching occurred in 1998.[1]

Grand Saline doesn't have the same proven historical record as
Jasper or Vidor. The only thing that makes the town unique is its
stories of white supremacy. The perception is entirely constructed
from these tales—not anything else.

THE CULTURAL POWER OF STORYTELLING

Before looking at the specific ways storytelling denotes white supremacy in Grand Saline, it's important to understand the ways
in which storytelling can rhetorically be a tool of liberation and
oppression. While research in rhetoric and composition and other
fields has examined the rhetoric of storytelling in various capaci-
ties (especially in North American Indigenous [NAI] and Latinx
communities and in terms of "counterstories," as I explain below),
I examine this practice from a different perspective: by applying a
critical race theory lens to the way white people tell racialized stories in my hometown to see how the storytelling maintains white
supremacy. I refer to this act as *hegemonic storytelling*. Whereas NAI
scholars have often analyzed storytelling using a cultural-rhetorics
methodology to attribute to it a resistance to Eurocentric logic (a

different form of white supremacy), I aim to show how storytelling becomes a means of community building and knowledge production that aids a culture of white supremacy. Storytelling not only exists as means for marginalized people to construct counter-communities in relation to those in power, but it is also how some hegemonic communities construct their own identities and keep marginalizing others. In Grand Saline, I argue, people tell racialized, hegemonic stories about their past to preserve white supremacy.

In his book *The Truth about Stories*, Thomas King, a Canadian First Nations Indigenous writer and scholar, characterizes North American Indigenous storytelling as unique, claiming, "For Native storytellers, there is generally a proper place and time to tell a story. Some are only told in the winter when snow is on the ground or during certain ceremonies or at specific moments in a season" (153). King embodies these characteristics of "properness" in his own chapters, using specific Indigenous stories to reflect the purpose of stories in our daily lives. Though King's purview is not directly planted in the subfield of NAI rhetorics, his work teaches us about the importance of storytelling as a cultural art form and has become the impetus of much research in rhetoric and composition and NAI studies over the past fifteen years. In her rhetoric and composition dissertation, *Listening to Our Stories in Dusty Boxes*, Emily Legg adds to King's discussion by framing Indigenous storytelling as

> participatory networks that situate stories within indigenous views of ecologies and outside of the traces of Eurocentric understandings of stories. Practiced in the *sgadug*,[2] storytelling as *gagoga*[3] creates a process where no one person becomes the authority or knowledge producer, but all work together to keep the community strong by telling stories that share knowledge. (39)

Legg describes NAI storytelling as providing an entire community agency, whereby no one person is the expert and all can share in building community and producing knowledge. Instead of focusing on storytelling in the storyteller-audience binary, as with Eurocentric traditions, NAI storytelling affords everyone agency in the customary form. This marks NAI storytelling as inherently community based.

In the introduction to their edited collection *Survivance, Sovereignty, and Story*, Lisa King, Rose Gubele, and Joyce Rain Anderson contend that colonial logic often silences Indigenous storytelling traditions. Indigenous people must preserve the practice, the editors say, because stories "tell us who we are, locate us in time and space and history and land, and suggest who gets to speak and how" (3). The editors open their collection by emphasizing these power dynamics because of how they stifle scholarly interest. Just as Victor Villanueva tells us that colonial discourse creates hierarchies of knowledge creation ("On the Rhetoric and Precedents of Racism," 656), and we must break precedent in order to accept other cultural forms (similar to the way white supremacy hinders other racial discourses), King, Gubele, and Anderson demonstrate that NAI storytelling traditions should not be disregarded simply because they do not fit into Eurocentric rhetorical practices. Whereas Thomas King and Legg focus on the specific attributes of Indigenous storytelling, Lisa King, Gubele, and Anderson and Villanueva pinpoint how such cultural traditions deserve renewed emphasis because of their marginalized status.

Many scholars embody the resistance to colonial logic in their academic texts. In his introduction to *American Indian Rhetorics of Survivance*, Ernest Stromberg writes that many of the contemporary analyses in his book are about bridging American Indian traditions with colonized traditions. He continues:

> For this reason, a number of the authors in this collection examine the ways in which Native rhetoricians appropriate the language, styles, and beliefs of their white audiences in order to establish a degree of consubstantiality. Across divides of language, beliefs, and traditions, Native rhetoricians have had to find ways to make their voices heard and respected by a too frequently uninterested and even hostile audience. Thus, in the post-contact rhetoric of Native North Americans, one finds an acute awareness of audience. (6)

This consubstantiality is embedded within the various stories told in the book. For instance, in Richard Clark Eckert's "Wennebojo Meets a 'Real Indian,'" Eckert presents the narrative of Wennebojo as he discusses with fellow Indians what constitutes Indianness and ends the story by stating that "a person symbolizes a real Indian by *being* a real Indian" (emphasis mine, 271). The purpose of the narrative is to decolonize and decentralize Eurocentric logic.

However, others, such as Aman Sium and Eric Ritskes, posit that we should never essentialize NAI storytelling acts; the practices vary from each location and tribe to the next. At the same time, they agree that decoloniality remains vital to this tradition, writing, "Indigenous storytelling works to both deconstruct colonial ways of coming to know, as well as construct alternatives. . . . [These stories are] grounded in rootedness and relationality" (viii). Thus, if we *do* mold these traditions into a collective, we can pinpoint how they resist colonization through bringing in the personal, emphasizing space and place, and focusing on community building and relationships. NAI peoples construct knowledge and replicate it via their customs, and by bringing these traditions back into the open, illustrating that they have existed since long before colonizers settled in this country, NAI scholars actively resist the accepted modes of knowledge creation.

NAI scholars are not the only ones illustrating the cultural powers of storytelling. Latinx scholars such as Aja Martinez and Carl Gutiérrez-Jones display similar traditions in Latinx histories and practices. Specifically, Martinez has used her *counterstories* (more on that term below) to illustrate her struggles as a young Latina woman in Arizona dealing with language discrimination, racist stereotypes, and making it in academia ("A Plea" and "Alejandra Writes a Book"). Her narratives parallel those of other Latinx scholars in the field, such as Villanueva, who have used personal stories to illustrate the hardships of growing up Brown and weaving through the obstacle course of academia. Similarly, in his book *Rethinking the Borderlands*, Gutiérrez-Jones explains how Chicanx narratives "resist hegemonic assumptions about reading" (25) and need to be "historically situated on the margin . . . which must contend with refashioning their positions from within a field of Anglo institutional forces" (33). *Rethinking the Borderlands* concludes with a major claim:

> In the Chicano narratives we discover a pattern of linguistic inquiry parallel to that undertaken by Bakhtin. Chicano artists have of course pursued this inquiry with the dictates of their own social context at the forefront of their efforts. Hence, their specific reworkings of historical events and legal culture have, among other things, posited legal rhetoric as a set of structuring principles for performances in which the Anglo society's racist actions may cloak themselves in postures of judicial neutrality. (169)

To Gutiérrez-Jones, Chicanx narratives have attempted to challenge the neutrality of judicial rhetoric to show that no frameworks are ever truly neutral. They often have a specific (Anglo) lens.

Juan C. Guerra connects these narrative approaches to acts of identity in his book *Language, Culture, Identity, and Citizenship in College Classrooms and Communities*, specifically focusing on issues of language usage, the problem of "Mexicanness," and ethnic appearance. Even in talking about these issues, Guerra takes a narrative approach, sharing his own personal stories as a means to further illustrate identity issues for Latinx peoples. Cruz Medina expands these narratives to digital platforms via a Latinx storytelling tradition, *testimonio*, or a narrative that attempts to inspire social change (Beverley). Medina sees digital *testimonio* as offering "perspectives on experiences for communities that have traditionally been observed and mediated without many opportunities to voice their own experiences." All of these scholars from Villanueva and Martinez to Guerra and Medina use storytelling either to convey aspects of Latinx identity or to embody Latinx perspectives via specific storytelling traditions.

The ways that Native American Indigenous and Latinx peoples construct their own storytelling traditions demonstrate the power minority cultures have in defining their own means of knowledge-creation and community. Similarly, recent scholarship from critical race theorists and rhetoricians finds that storytelling can also be used to combat power structures, through the use of "counterstorytelling." *Counterstorytelling* is defined as storytelling that builds community and shared understanding through challenging "received wisdom" and master narratives (Delgado 2414). For instance, a Black woman who shares her story of being a single mother while also being a successful lawyer would combat negative images of Black single mothers being "welfare queens" (a trope popularized by President Ronald Reagan in the 1980s).[4] Therefore, counterstorytelling attempts to subvert negative narratives of minoritized populations. While Richard Delgado theorized this term in a 1989 article on the use of undermining racist perceptions in the courtroom, recent work by Aja Martinez and Frankie Condon illustrates how these stories work rhetorically.

While I explored Martinez's work as it fits into Latinx traditions, I want to also show how she's expanding critical race theory. Martinez's 2014 article "A Plea for Critical Race Theory Counterstory" argues that "counterstory functions as a method for marginalized people to intervene in research methods that would form master narratives based on ignorance and on assumptions about minoritized peoples like Chican@s" (53). Her article challenges the use of personal narrative in our field and demonstrates, by embodying her own academic counterstory, how people might use autoethnographic frameworks as means to challenge racial stereotypes. Overall, Martinez contends that these types of narratives can alter racial power dynamics simply by undercutting tropes against racialized peoples. More recently, her book *Counterstory: The Rhetoric and Writing of Critical Race Theory* makes an argument for how counterstory should be better used in rhetoric and composition studies via analyses of narrated dialogues, fantasy/allegories, autobiographical reflections, and dialogic epistles. She does this "to provide a fuller sense of how the tools (methods) of CRT shape the rhetorical efficacy of counterstory," and the various analyses and counterstories she provides along the ways illustrate how the personal can be scholarly and vice versa. This book advances narrative scholarship from scholars such as Condon, who make arguments about whiteness and the performative narratives that are constructed as vestiges (or fake vestiges) of antiracism. In her book *I Hope I Join the Band,* Condon notes the power of counterstorytelling (without explicitly using the term), stating that "critical race theorists have long used the practice of storytelling to trouble or destabilize claims to universality" (141). Both Martinez and Condon emphasize how counterstories attempt to resist master narratives by embodying practices, reversing stereotypes, and opposing universality. They illustrate that minority communities have the means to form their own groups through storytelling, and that they can also use these stories to flip power structures and bigoted tropes.

I discuss NAI and Latinx storytelling and counterstorytelling to illustrate how stories have been talked about in our field recently and to show them as liberating rhetorical practices. However, storytelling isn't a neutral practice. Certain storytelling traditions can actually *maintain* power or *sustain* dominant narratives. Michael Bamberg, a psychologist who studies identity and narrative, says that speakers and audiences formulate narratives that either become "complicit" with or "counter" dominant discourses (352). Thus speakers can view their stories as maintaining a narrative or countering it, and audiences can do the same. Some people call dominant discourses "master narratives"—especially in critical race theory terms—or narratives that "mute, erase, and neutralize features of racial struggle in ways that reinforce ideologies of White supremacy" (Woodson 317). These narratives work in terms of race and other forms of identity and oppression as well. Master narratives don't necessarily imply intent, either; people can reinforce dominant narratives without knowing that they do so. Critical race theorists—such as Christine A. Stanley, Martinez, and Daniel G. Solórzano and Tara J. Yosso—employ the term *master narratives* to suggest how stories can be used as a means to subjugate on individual and systemic levels.

Master narratives maintain norms and hegemony simply by reproducing stories that suggest that their view of the world is correct. So, for instance, some people believe that minorities are less intelligent than white people, and use stories—be they personal anecdotes or racist generalizations—to make these claims. These stories thus oppress people of color because they label them as less than and also keep white people in a superior status. In this sense, stories can be used to sustain normative discourse, to keep the status quo intact. As Eduardo Bonilla-Silva notes in *Racism without Racists* when discussing affirmative action (policies that attempt to challenge the norm), white people often share stories of someone they know who lost a job to a person of color because of affirmative action. Though Bonilla-Silva doesn't emphasize the narrative formation in his research, his argument illustrates how white people will construct narratives to maintain structures that work to their advantage or normal ways of life for them. Of course, these stories are mostly fabrications, because what sort of employer or school announces that their new hire/student was an affirmative action case? Why does a white audience assume that affirmative action was involved? Nonetheless, these narratives attempt to keep order and can still have detrimental effects for people of color. I refer to these narratives as hegemonic stories to highlight both the way these stories maintain the status quo while also emphasizing how they oppress people of color as well.

As displayed in the previous chapter, the people in Grand Saline use this different storytelling tradition, a network of white supremacist tales in which no one is the authority but in which all citizens have agency in spreading and maintaining bigotry, to fashion themselves as white supremacists or as people who feel fine being associated with white supremacy. Recent research demonstrates how people have employed storytelling to push against normative narratives and to reinforce ideologies, and my analysis adds to this by demonstrating how *majority* groups form their own communities and use stories embedded with white supremacy to preserve their culture. These stories and public memories keep the perception of Grand Saline as racist intact because they position some to believe that racism still controls the community—whether residents agree or not. In this sense, the truth behind these stories does not matter because the circulation of these tales and their rhetorical value *become* the town's reality.

A LEGACY OF RACIST STORYTELLING

Most people I interviewed for this project were asked about the stories in Grand Saline, especially if they were from Grand Saline, still lived there, or lived in a neighboring community. (The only people not asked about these stories were some colleagues of Moore's who wouldn't necessarily know much about the town.) Every single person I asked about these stories, roughly fifty people in total, could name at least one of the three tales.[5] All people in Grand Saline could describe some version of the Poletown and sundown-town stories, with most being able to discuss the Clark's Ferry one as well. Most people from neighboring communities could name the sundown-town stories but didn't always know the Poletown and Clark's Ferry stories. Still, I am less interested in the fact that these people recall these various artifacts of folklore than I am intrigued by *how* and *why* they recall them.

The Poletown Bridge was the most vivid story for most residents. Some residents, such as Shirley Crawford, a mixed-race twenty-year-old with Black lineage, remembered being told that "they would sometimes torture [Black people] by throwing rocks at them, cutting them, or making them watch their other family members die before they [were lynched]." Crawford distinctly remembers hearing these tales from peers who would laugh about it. She states that she would often laugh rather than cry because she did not want people to know how much the story bothered her. Since this story had sinister undertones, it drove Crawford to dissociate from white people in the town because she made connections between these stories and how her white friends felt about Black people. Others in town, such as Chet Yant, a white elder in the community who died in 2018, corroborate hearing such terrible stories about the bridge: "Oh sure, they used to take Black people there and would hang them and then cut off their heads. Now I've never seen this myself, but I just ask, 'Why? Why?'" Yant believes the story was true.

However, not everyone considers these stories as historical fact. Other residents, like Amanda Jones, a thirty-year-old white woman, recall the space of the Poletown Bridge a bit differently. Jones states, "I believe the name 'Poletown' originated from where Black people would be [hanged] by members of the KKK on poles in 'Poletown.' Once again I believe these are just stories. My great grandparents and grandparents lived in [Grand Saline] for decades and never saw or knew of these happenings." She continues, "I remember [these stories] when I was younger and I guess they were told when I was in high school, but I'm not positive. I guess [these stories are retold for] the same reason any fucked-up story gets told over and over again: it's a part of the town's history, and perhaps it's a way for people to remember how things once were." Jones acknowledges the tale of Poletown but does not necessarily believe it means the town has a racist past. However, she still connects the story to "a way for people to remember how things once were," suggesting that people fondly recall these horrific memories because they remind them of when racism was normalized. She implicitly associates the racism embedded within the story with the white supremacist views of some in the community. Her memories are important because they reflect what the majority of Grand Saline feels: the site is seen as having been racialized in the past but not linked to any wrongdoing in the present (though she does make this connection and doesn't see it).

The actual story of Poletown serves to dehumanize Black people. Since virtually no Black people live in town and most residents do not engage with Black people on a daily basis, townsfolks' relationship to their Black brethren and sistren is limited to this story—which rhetorically defines Black people as victims and as products of white violence. In his article "That Camera Won't Save You!," Armond R. Towns refers to the process of capturing "antiBlack violence" on body cameras as normalizing "the commodification of Black deaths" through the process of making them into for-profit memes. A similar process occurs in Grand Saline, with the story of Poletown being its own meme of sorts, where white people profit from being at the top of the racial hierarchy, the agents of violence who tell stories about racial violence. Also, the dehumanization of Black people in the Poletown story parallels the dehumanization of Black people often heard in high school and other places around town (Sam Adams claims she heard Black people being called "n------" and "monkeys" almost every day in high school). Thus, white supremacy thrives not only in the explicit decrees of bigotry but also in how white people tell stories of Black victimhood.

Whereas mostly everyone had clear memories of Poletown, the recollections of what Clark's Ferry represents were a bit more muddied, though a racial perspective was typically present. Adams recalls that "Clark's Ferry is a ghost story about the area." After remembering the origin of the story, she declares, "There are also stories about the KKK and Clark's Ferry. They say that the KKK used that area to torture and kill countless Black men and women. They say you can hear their screams, often likened to the sound of a panther screaming." Adams recognizes the KKK narrative, and her language also confirms how KKK influences Grand Saline residents—by aligning them with the hate group through the storytelling act. By recognizing this story and associating it with racial pain and hatred, Adams shows how commonplace white supremacy is within the traditions of Grand Saline. Other adult respondents, such as Tracy Lunsford, another mid-twenties white woman, reiterate this point by explicitly acknowledging the association between town members and the KKK. "Everyone knows of the KKK in the area," Lunsford claims. "Their presence is just everywhere. Anyone who knows of Grand Saline knows that the KKK is here." By noting the KKK's continual presence, interviewees like Lunsford and Adams establish how white supremacy thrives through associating the two with one another. They also illustrate that the legend of the KKK influences the way Black people interact with the town (because they believe these stories) and the way residents construct their own identities in relation to this hate group. The KKK story thus aligns people with white supremacy by rhetorically connecting the entire community to the extremist organization.

Some residents interpret the story of Clark's Ferry as a joke or tall tale and believe the KKK does not have any influence in Grand Saline. "It's just an old wise [sic] tale, and nothing else," states city administrator Rex White, an older white man. "It was just a way for boys to sneak off and scare young girls." Other residents believe, historically, the KKK had a major presence in the area but contend the town has moved past its bigotry. B. R. Fite, a middle-aged white publisher of the town newspaper, says that the KKK would never be allowed to march in town anymore because the town does not want them: "We got it. We have a Black president.[6] Come on. They aren't welcome here anymore." His position parallels what many think about this story: it is part of the town's past, and it has no bearing on the present. While older residents often try to distance the community from these tales, rhetorically speaking, the distancing accomplishes nothing. Still, many Black interviewees believe Grand Saline has a KKK problem because they hear and share these same stories as truth. Michael McClendon, a Black thirty-some-year-old former resident of Van, Texas, a town ten miles south of Grand Saline, puts it bluntly: "We've all heard these stories before, and many Black people are afraid of Grand Saline because of its association with the KKK." The stories' power stems from how they are shared, discursively.

Since so many Grand Saline residents know of Clark's Ferry and repeat these stories to others, the storytelling act bolsters the hatred in the community, even if unintentionally. People consistently associate the KKK with Grand Saline and Grand Saline with the KKK—as one lawyer put it, "The Klan doesn't have to be public in Grand Saline anymore" because the two parallel one another—which produces a symbiotic relationship between them. While different residents apply different motivations to these stories (again being that they might be jokes, or explicit racism, or "history"), the continual discussion of the KKK's being active at Clark's Ferry sustains such a narrative. The reality of the KKK in Grand Saline is not as important as its symbolic link to the town.

I was embedded within this racist memory when I took part in the prank at the Clark's Ferry site. Though at first I viewed my actions as unrelated to the memory of the area, in retrospect I see that I was clearly wrong. Even the people we pranked imagined that perhaps we were associated with the KKK simply because that site symbolizes the meeting space for the infamous racist group. The two cannot be untangled. Even now, over fifteen years later, I wonder if my friends are still comfortable with our actions. I wonder if they would, again, just refer to this all as a "joke" and hide behind the pretense that jokes have no consequences.

Finally, where nonresidents I spoke with knew only a bit about Clark's Ferry and Poletown (they were more likely to talk about the KKK and lynchings in more general terms), many of them acknowledged hearing stories of the sundown town and being afraid of Grand Saline because of this status. This was the most common story nonresidents could recite. For instance, Lucy Winters, a young Black woman who grew up in Edgewood, a town ten miles west of Grand Saline, says with a sense of certainty, "I do believe I heard there was a sign in Grand Saline that stated, 'N-----, don't let the sun go down on you here!'" She claims she always felt afraid to drive through the community because of this story. James Woods, an older Black man from the Van area, makes this point clearer: "They used to beat Black people there when they caught them there after dark. . . . [Even now] when heading to a town on the other side of Grand Saline, if I could jump over the town, I would. . . . You can't just erase the things that happened in Grand Saline." To both of these nearby residents, the story of the sundown town emerges as a warning of what might happen to them if they come to Grand Saline. A former white news reporter for the county, Leon Sylvester, says that while many outsiders believe these signs were real, people in Grand Saline feel differently. He asserts, "Most people in Grand Saline, however, seemed to deny the sign's existence and would not talk about it when asked. A number of people I spoke with, however, were certain of having seen it at some point in the past." For many people outside of Grand Saline, the stories of the sundown town signs are told as truth, arguably as a means for survival, though people in town often refute their existence.

Still, everyone in town has heard the stories—even if they disagree with them—and mostly claim outsiders are to blame for their perceptions of racism. One former resident, a young white woman, Lacey Michaels, recalls "being told, mostly by people from surrounding towns, that Grand Saline used to have a sign at the city limits." Other residents, young and old, such as Sam Adams,

Wayne Sloan, Diana Wilt, and Becky Veach, agree to hearing about these signs from friends and people in neighboring communities but never saw them with their own eyes. However, Yant dissents from most of the town and claims that he saw the signs and knew a friend who owned one of them (though he did not specify whom). "I bet the other sign is hanging in someone's game room here in town," he posits. Some on social media have claimed seeing the sign as late as the 1970s.

Again, just as with the stories of Poletown and Clark's Ferry, the story of the sundown signs configures the people in Grand Saline as identifying with white supremacy. However, this time, the stories demonstrate how people outside of the community construct a racist perception of Grand Saline, which puts people in town on the defensive. "We don't have to continue to talk about the stories of Poletown and the sundown signs," White contended when asked about the stories of Grand Saline. "If you don't watch out, this talk will get all of this [stories of racism] started again, and we don't want to do that." His words echo a position many people in Grand Saline maintain—that they must defend their town against people claiming they are racist rather than taking the time to address and reconcile such claims.

White's position contradicts the story I heard in the coffee shop when asking about the sundown town signs. Most Grand Saline residents interviewed about the town were quick to claim that outsiders were the ones telling these stories and keeping the legacy of racism alive, but the old man in the coffee shop who quickly—and without hesitation—told me the "joke" about the old sheriff terrorizing Black people who were caught in town proves that this isn't just a phenomenon cultivated by neighboring communities. If this domino player was this quick to tell me the sheriff story, in front of a film crew, do we truly believe that he would not be telling other Grand Saline residents the same tale from time to time?

Of course, we cannot essentialize the people in Grand Saline and suggest that they all believe that racism is behind them or that they all truly don't tell stories of their racist legacy, but my research suggests that there are many residents who still feel comfortable spreading these stories publicly and privately too.

MAINTAINING WHITE SUPREMACY

While the section above pinpoints the rhetorical legacy of hegemonic storytelling in Grand Saline and fleshes out its narratives—
making some claims about why these stories are told and how they
affect audiences—we can summarize how members of Grand Saline preserve white supremacy through three rhetorical moves embedded within their stories: (1) using ambiguity and stock formulas
to hide white supremacist viewpoints; (2) taking defensive stances
against people referring to the town as racist via *apophasis*; and (3)
constituting themselves as white supremacists via their histories and
stories—even if they say those histories and stories aren't real. Not
all of these moves are obvious in every interview conducted with
residents of Grand Saline, but nonetheless they exist as the key rhetorical tools that create a white supremacist bond for storytellers
and audiences.

First, the hegemonic storytelling in Grand Saline remains a
type of tradition that has been passed along for well over a century. Charles Moore acknowledged this tradition in his letter to the
town (he remembered hearing stories of lynchings in the 1940s). I
took part in this tradition during the early 2000s, and many people
I know still recite these stories today. Amy Heuman and Catherine
Langford argue that rhetorically "traditions are customs and practices handed down from the predecessor. Tradition is not observed;
tradition is enacted" (126). The people of Grand Saline "enact"
these traditions by memorializing them in the storytelling process
and keeping them in the public sphere through repetition. Kids
and younger adults typically are the agents in the storytelling act
because they use them as cultural capital, and elders in the community attempt to stop them from hurting the town's image. As
Diana Wilt, a white woman in her late twenties, stated to me, "Kids
in Grand Saline learn about these stories at a very young age. And
they repeat them throughout their entire lives, through high school
and afterward." Jose Garcia, a Mexican American man I graduated
with, went even further: "You hear them all the time in Grand
Saline but especially in high school. On any given weekend night,
you could be out with friends and would hear about one of these
stories." While adults do tell these stories, high schoolers are the

arbiters of the ritual. They tell them for various reasons, but as Adams and Garcia demonstrate, and as some of the older men attest, the kids in high school are the ones mostly spreading them. This is how the tradition forms. High schoolers consistently pass these stories down from one generation to the next. Thus, the stories pervade the entire community because they are traditionally repeated by *all* younger folk, meaning that even most of the elders in the community were agents in keeping this tradition alive at one point in their lives, even if they don't do so now. Though many elders in the community attempt to move past the town's white supremacist perception—or argue that they do—many younger adults and kids reinforce bigotry via this hegemonic storytelling.

Of course, it is impossible to truly understand the multitudes of reasons behind why people in Grand Saline share these stories. From the interviews I explored above, some people argue that these narratives are told as jokes, as way for adults and teenagers to "scare" one another in a playful way. Other people claim they are a part of Grand Saline's oral history tradition; they believe these stories represent the history of the town and view the storytelling act as simply that of replaying history. Finally, there are those in town with more liberal ideologies, who hear these tales and argue that they reflect the town's white supremacy. Different people in different occasions tell these stories for different reasons. Some people do want to explicitly spread a white supremacist agenda; others believe they are simply reciting historical truths or are just joking with their peers. In the preservation of white supremacy, these motives hardly matter because the perception of Grand Saline is that of a racist society. The *idea* of Grand Saline being a white supremacist community erases all other intents and motives of storytellers because whenever outsiders hear these stories, they typically don't question the motives; they use them as evidence that Grand Saline is still racist.

White supremacist ideology thus hides behind the ambiguous motives of storytelling in Grand Saline. While most town members would not qualify themselves as white supremacists, their stories affect outsiders in nearby towns and across the state differently. Yet if anyone tells residents that these stories are racist, they can respond by stating that they are just jokes or stories and have no ill intent, which allows ambiguity to be used as a defense. They apply the deliberate ambiguity of motives as a means to tell racist stories. I am sure many of the storytellers wouldn't admit to being racist (we can parse what that means but that is what they would claim); but I am also positive there are many people who tell the stories as a means of expressing racism, and if called out, they employ the strategic-ambiguity defense to mask their true intents.

Similarly, the stories are *topoi*—or commonplaces—that function as stock formulas for racist thought and ideology—flexible enough for people to argue about them as neutral at times while also being an explicit indicator for white supremacy at other times. In classical rhetoric, *topoi* were the bank of arguments that a speaker could use on any occasion. However, we can extrapolate this notion to see how the commonplace nature of white supremacist stories in Grand Saline provides a space to hide racist ideology. Since these stories are embedded within the nature of the town, everyone knows them and can recite them with ease. However, this allows them to argue that such stories don't contain or sustain a particular racist viewpoint—even when the stories themselves are unambiguously racist—because they argue that everyone knows them and they are just stories they tell for no reason. They use the commonplace nature of these stories as a means to defend themselves. "We all know these stories; therefore they are meaningless" is the argument. Nonetheless, these stories are also told to other people to scare them or to illustrate racism (the football player sharing the Poletown story with me, for instance). Their commonplace nature makes them adaptable enough to conceal motives.

Hall, a few months after writing his article "Man on Fire," told me that "where there is smoke there is usually fire. Grand Saline is known as one of the most racist towns in the state of Texas but there does not seem to be much history to back up that claim." Hall's characterization of the town corresponds with my own argument: the actual history of Grand Saline's racism is not exceptional, but the storytelling *is* exceptional in the way that it constructs white supremacy for the citizens of the town. I believe we should look at this metaphor differently: the fire, in this sense, is not the historically substantiated proof of white supremacy that Hall researched; rather, it is the *ideology* of white supremacy. The smoke, the hegemonic storytelling within Grand Saline, then does not corroborate historical truth; it corroborates an ideology. White supremacy lives in Grand Saline—in part—because its ideology and storytelling tradition persist.

Second, the rhetorical moves that Grand Saline residents use in defending their community also, by extension, defend white supremacy. The community protects itself against being characterized as evil or racist because they do not fashion themselves as racists and believe any such label essentializes their community. In the interviews I conducted with Grand Saline residents, many respondents took an obviously defensive approach: "I'm sure there are people in this town who are still racist, but if you can find me a town that doesn't have racists, I'll say, 'Look, a town, an amazing town, without racists,'" claims Lisa Morrison, head of the Main Street Project. "We have to get over all this bull crap [on the history of Grand Saline] and just say the KKK aren't welcome anymore," states Fite. "All this myth and legend is just that, and we shouldn't keep talking about it. We should focus on the recorded history," asserts Elvis Allen. Each of these encounters, in one way or another, is a defensive strategy employed by town members to push against perceptions of their racism. Of course, some of these defensive strategies have logic. Who doesn't want to defend their own community? Or understand the split between unverified stories and history? Or acknowledge that racism exists in every town?

They still affiliate themselves as defenses of white supremacy. Their defenses range from critiquing the storytelling as being false, to saying that the KKK are the only bearers of racism (not the community), to arguing that racists are everywhere so this problem isn't unique. Instead of focusing on ways to move forward, most of these people rely on trite excuses that uphold and shield their community more than they attempt to speak to "truth." More important, they suggest that others' perception of them doesn't matter, and if they just pretend it isn't there then it will get better.

This move is known as *apophasis*. Apophasis is a rhetorical tactic in which an individual denies speaking to something while, actually, speaking to said subject. This move has made its way into the public sphere recently thanks to Donald Trump, who uses the move quite often. For instance, when Trump criticized Jeb Bush in January 2018 on the primary trail, he told a crowd, "I was going to say 'dummy' Bush; I won't say it. I won't say it" (Bobic). Trump's use, clearly, isn't that clever, and his "denial" is obviously a sham because he does want to call Bush a "dummy." A more tactful use of apophasis dates back to Cicero's "Pro Caelio" speech, a speech given in defense of Marcus Caelius Rufus, who was charged with the attempted murder of Dio of Alexandria and the attempted poisoning of Clodia. In the speech, Cicero takes aim at Clodia, saying: "Clodia, I am not thinking now of the wrong you have done to me. I am putting to one side the memory of humiliation. I pass over your cruel treatment of my family while I was away. Consider that nothing I have said has been said against you." In arguing that he said nothing "against" her, Cicero also charges her of wronging him and treating his family poorly, and he does so much more skillfully than does Trump.

Members of Grand Saline consistently employ apophasis as a defense of their community. They say that we shouldn't talk about Grand Saline's reputation because it will bring up all their racist problems again, yet, by saying we shouldn't talk about it, they are actively taking a side in defending their town. They tell us where they fall on the racism debate—they believe it isn't a problem anymore. This creates a rhetorical bubble that can't be burst. Anyone who talks about the racism problem openly is wrong and is stirring up trouble, and anyone who denies bringing up the racist stories can take to defending the town without much opposition. Apophasis gives the town a built-in defense whereby they can speak to the town's racism through denying it.

These protective strategies reiterate the color-blind racism that Bonilla-Silva writes about in *Racism without Racists*. In his text,

Bonilla-Silva expounds on the ways white America uses coded language and arguments to employ racism without seeming overtly racist. Expanding on this taxonomy of color-blind racism, I argue that these defensive moves become rhetorical aids of white supremacy as well because they shift blame to people decrying racism rather than focusing on the community's abundant issues. These defenses fail to recognize the problems in the community.

However, a few people I interviewed acknowledged that the community needs to do some soul searching to better understand why outsiders often view them as racist. Emily Erwin puts it this way: "I feel like we have to say, 'I feel like I'm not racist, but maybe I should listen to what people have to say.' Listen to why they say we are racist. Listen to them explain why they think we are racist. Really listen. And if then we feel like we are not racist, okay.'" However, people like Erwin are in the minority compared to those who want to simply turn to defensive positions. The majority protects white supremacy because they would rather take the defensive approach than interrogate the realities of their situation. They would rather say, "No, all of this is false," than question why this perception problem has existed for over a hundred years. They associate themselves with protecting white supremacy because they care more about their tarred image than tackling the issues behind their perceived bigotry in the first place. Even though their defensive strategy seems reasonable in many ways, to Black people in nearby towns, like Michael McClendon, it just shows that nothing will change. Apophasis becomes the signal that insiders can use to defend the town publicly.

Last, these stories expand upon constitutive rhetorics, or rhetoric that demonstrates the ways groups and communities establish themselves, be it via language practices, legal procedures and proceedings, or cultural practices. Christa Olson discusses these formations in her book *Constitutive Visions*, in which she illustrates how Ecuadorian national identity constructs arguments of both popular and national sovereignty. Her book demonstrates the various "rhetorical strategies of nation making in Ecuador" (131) and argues that the nature of one's sovereignty depends upon "the same constitutive relations that drive national identification" (198). Gregory Clark has made similar arguments about constitutive rhetorics and American landscapes, arguing that such rhetorics, in this case of landscapes and tourist sites, constitute national identity. Some scholarship even indicates the way constitutive rhetoric can *fail* to build a community (Zagacki). However, these constitutive issues are a bit different when we think about communities that align around white supremacy. In their argument about *The Turner Diaries* (a book often interpreted as a mouthpiece for white supremacy), Charles Goehring and George N. Dionisopoulos have argued how the book not only establishes white supremacy for its target audience but also how it might become a justification for its audience to engage in violence (384).

Though many Grand Saline residents would argue that they are not white supremacist, their stories and histories constitute them as such. At the earliest, stories about Grand Saline's racial transgressions began in 1909. In an article from the *Grand Saline Sun* that year, the editor reported on a story of a massacre of Black people occurring out at the salt flats in the late 1800s and believed that bodies of the dead could be spread out on the ground to cover the entire area. The editor wrote:

> When the [Civil War] closed negroes were in the majority in Grand Saline—being known then as Jordan Saline. . . . But when the surrender came and the negro was set free many of them were left here by the white people and this resulted in the negro getting a treatment which has kept him away from here until this day. Those who know something of tohse [sic] days say that there were enough dead negroes thrown into the lake on the Saline prairie for the bones to line its entire bottom.

This evidence, only printed in a newspaper, is secondhand, but it adds to the dimension of Grand Saline's public memory and tradition. It is not far-fetched to believe that poor Black workers were displaced by poor white workers around the turn of the century in the area. This corresponds with James Loewen's research and with other testimonies gathered from townsfolk, such as Don Vickery, an elderly friend of Moore, who claimed his father was a constable during this time and told stories about a salt mine strike leading to a massacre of Black people. With these changes, fights, deaths, and possible massacres could take place. Local historian Allen dismisses this account completely as sensationalism, claiming that it was fabricated to sell papers.[7] Nonetheless, the *idea* that Grand Saline has a racist culture problem has existed since at least 1909, a bit over a century ago.

Fast-forward to the 1940s and 1950s, when Charles Moore was an adolescent in Grand Saline, and he heard similar stories about Poletown, stories that many people in Grand Saline would know today. Moore wrote in his final letter to Grand Saline, "When I was about 10-years-old, some friends and I were walking down the road toward the creek to catch some fish, when a man called 'Uncle Billy' stopped us and called us into his house for a drink of water—but his real purpose was to cheerily tell us about helping to kill 'n------' and put their heads up on a pole [in Poletown]." Sixty years before I was in high school, some forty-five years before I was even born, a young Moore had dealt with the public perception of racism in Grand Saline.

Fast-forward to my moving to Grand Saline in the early 2000s, and my own memories and upbringing in town evince the rhetorical plasticity of these tales: I heard all three of the major stories and participated in telling them. I am guilty of keeping these racist stories, and white supremacy, thriving in the town by sharing these tales as jokes, revealing them to outsiders, and believing on some level that, I, the Brown kid who wanted to be white, was superior to Black people. But most important, the evidence from the newspaper, Moore's letter, my own memories, and interviews with residents in Grand Saline highlight how the values entrenched within these stories are inherently rhetorical.

Even if people in Grand Saline do not want to recognize it publicly, the white supremacist stories constitute their culture and their fiber. Their ancestors created a space to believe that Black people were massacred in 1909. Their ancestors lynched at least one person in Poletown and decapitated him because of racism. Charles Moore heard the stories of these lynchings and the KKK in the 1940s and 1950s, illustrating that the stories had become part of the community's lore, and fifty years later, I heard tales of the same spaces and subjects. Stories like this wouldn't exist for over a century unless they held some communal properties for townsfolk. Though many residents of Grand Saline want to move past these stories because they cultivate a bad reputation for the town, that seems impossible, because passing on this folklore remains one of the major traditions for kids and young adults. It embodies part of the town's identity.

The stories constitute the town as white supremacist.

So what is Grand Saline to do?

The stories place the community in a seemingly impossible predicament: residents are damned if they tell these stories and damned if they don't. However, they also present Grand Saline with an opportunity to react publicly. As a researcher, I am unsure where I have agency in claiming what Grand Saline should or should not do (especially since many people I love still live in the community), and I do not claim to have all of the answers. Still, I believe two things could help: First, when people tell these stories, they typically are not looking for truth, nor do they stop others from repeating these stories. Never in my years in Grand Saline did someone attempt to say, "Well, the story of Clark's Ferry is complicated and usually racist." No one told kids not to spread these tales. Rather, it was accepted as truth for younger people, and there are many people in town, younger and older, who accept these stories as indicative of the community. Reconciliation can't occur in Grand Saline until people tell these stories by deconstructing them and sharing why the actions they describe are morally wrong. Second, the perceptions of Grand Saline as racist often held by outside communities will not change until residents systematically and publicly address these perceptions, because their silence, and the preponderance of storytelling, leaves outside communities to assume that nothing has changed. To combat this, the town needs to address these stories openly (perhaps through newspaper articles and community meetings) in order to change these perceptions.

White supremacy might perish if people attempted to start honest conversations about these stories.

If we are the products of the narratives we tell, then Grand Saline is a product of the white supremacy its narratives propagate—until, eventually, the town attempts to reconcile this.

White supremacy flourishes in Grand Saline through the act of hegemonic storytelling, just one of many tools that builds a rhetoric of preservation for the town. Specific stories about the town's racism, including stories about a lynching bridge, the KKK meeting at Clark's Ferry, and the sundown-town signs, create a space where the content of racist storytelling becomes central to the community's public memory and identity. Rhetorically, hegemonic storytelling embodies white supremacy for Grand Saline because it controls perception, constitutes the town's identity, and becomes a commonplace argument flexible enough to hide intent behind ideology. The act of hegemonic storytelling in Grand Saline is an act of preservation, one that moves to keep white supremacy intact.

In a storytelling tradition that consistently and continually fashions Grand Saline as white supremacist, there is no room for dissent. Everyone tells the stories and knows of them and no one does anything to prevent their spread. Whereas individuals might feel as though they aren't racist or don't have racial biases, the stories they tell and the stories outsiders hear are what constructs perceptions of the town. Storytelling doesn't just build collective identity, as many believe—it also perpetuates how outsiders perceive collectives.

When Thomas King writes, "The truth about stories is that is all that we are," he's right. He uses this to mean that our interactions with the world, the ways we understand ourselves, are built from stories. However, the pronoun *we* could easily be changed to *others* and still fit. The "truth" about *others* is that they are just stories too. True or untrue. How we observe who they are is through acts of storytelling.

Therefore, in a hegemonic storytelling tradition, where the only stories being told about a people make some into the oppressor and some into victims, how else could outside communities—and some people inside the community—perceive Grand Saline as a collective?

Let's end with another old adage: "When people show you who they are, you should believe them."

Yet when people tell stories of who they are, we're supposed to add caveats that they are just jokes or history?

We are supposed to . . . take them with a grain of salt?

5

"But Once Was Enough"

My Captain

The sparrow stood tall
Atop the wheelbarrow's bow
Chirping out his orders
Like an admiral at sea.

Would he dare pretend
More importance for himself
Than the oarsman aft
Who propels the weighty craft?
—Charles Moore

ON JUNE 23, 2014, CHARLES MOORE left his home in Allen, Texas, about thirty miles north of Dallas, and drove east, to his hometown of Grand Saline. He departed a bit after eight in the morning and arrived at the biggest parking lot in town, in front of the Dollar General and SophistiKutz salon, around ten. Mallie Munn, a stylist at the salon, stated she saw Moore arrive and figured he was just helping to pick up the weeds because he paced back and forth in the parking lot throughout the late morning and into the afternoon. Though she noticed his arrival and his presence, she didn't think about what he was doing (Morgan; Sanchez, *Man on Fire*).

Moore traversed the parking lot—taking a few breaks to go back inside his car—for seven hours. It's impossible to know exactly what he was thinking, but we do know a few facts: Moore had contemplated self-immolating for the past two days at Southern Methodist University (SMU) (Hood, *Passion*; Moore, "Last Appeal"). He claims that he wanted to do it on June 21 in honor of James Chaney, Andrew Goodman, and Michael Schwerner, who were murdered while attempting to register Black people to vote in rural Mississippi on June 21, 1964, fifty years to the day. (This case was infamously known as the "Freedom Summer Murders.") He respected the efforts of these men and viewed their deaths as the ultimate tragedy.

Moore didn't have Grand Saline as his first target, though; he wanted to complete his act on SMU's campus because he viewed the university's stance on homosexuality as an abomination in the twenty-first century ("Last Appeal"). He had long protested the policies of the Methodist Church—being kicked out of parishioners' houses for supporting integration in the 1950s and 1960s and having successfully protested the United Methodist Church's national convention in Austin, Texas, in 1995 (Hall, "Man on Fire"; Ward, "Methodist Minister"). Moore had committed to a fifteen-day hunger strike in 1995 to protest the national convention's stance on homosexuality. Because he was an advocate of gay and lesbian Christians in the greater Austin area, Moore's righteous indignation fed his protest acts. He always advocated for marginalized people, and he considered lighting himself on fire on SMU's campus to start a conversation about the church, the school, and LGBTQ+ rights.

Though Moore drove to the college campus twice to self-immolate, he could never do it. Moore's son, Guy, believes this is because he had too much admiration for the seminary school at SMU, of which he was a graduate, and didn't want to burden some of the people he truly respected who were still there. In a handwritten note at the bottom of "Last Appeal," Moore wrote, "Another day gone by—another failure—but it is hard to face the flames." He struggled with his decision.

So when Moore woke on June 23 after two unsuccessful self-immolations, he had a new destination in mind—his hometown.

What was he thinking?

What was he doing pacing back and forth in the parking lot for hours? Was he thinking about his family—his wife, children, and grandchildren? Was he thinking about what sort of press he assumed this sort of death would garner? Did he think about Chaney, Goodman, and Schwerner? Was he thinking about his own moments in Grand Saline? Was he praying to God? Was he trying to overcome his fears?

What was he thinking?

A little before 5:00 p.m., Moore grabbed a couch cushion from his car and walked a few feet away, closer to the highway, where he tossed it on the ground. Back at his car, he left behind his senior yearbook and circled his photo, so people could easily identify his body and understand that he was a former town resident. On his windshield, he also left a letter—"O Grand Saline, Repent of Your Racism"—that stated the reasons for his self-immolation: he wanted Grand Saline to ask for forgiveness for their past sins and to change their racist reputation in the present by being a more inclusive society. After detailing his personal experience of racism in the town in the 1940s and 1950s, he wrote:

> Many African Americans were lynched around here, probably some in Grand Saline: hanged, decapitated and burned, some while still alive. The vision of them haunts me greatly. So, at this late date, I have decided to join them by giving my body to be burned, with love in my heart not only for them but also for the perpetrators of such horror—but especially for the citizens of Grand Saline, many of whom have been very kind to me and others who may be moved to change the situation here. ("O Grand Saline")

The letter would be misinterpreted at first, by another stylist at the salon who skimmed it quickly while in shock. She would first tell people that evening that Moore killed himself because he felt guilty for being part of the KKK back in the day, and it would take a few days for his true motives to be seen by the public.

Moore dropped to his knees on the couch cushion and prepared himself for what would come next.

Why bring a couch cushion at all? It seems counterintuitive to desire comfort before choosing to burn yourself alive. What was the purpose of the cushion?

He fell to his knees and grabbed a small red gasoline container. He held it above his head and doused himself. "I just couldn't believe what he was doing," stated Munn. "I just told my friends watching it with me, 'That has to be water or something. . . . It has to be.'"

It wasn't.

What did it feel like to know you would be attempting to sacrifice yourself for a greater good in mere seconds? Did he have any regrets? Any second-guessing his decision?

"I saw him grab a large cigarette lighter that you would use for a barbecue grill . . . " remembered Buddy Lambert.

What do you have to be imagining in those final seconds? Do you just have hope that this could be the change the town needs?

" . . . and then he lit himself on fire, and he was covered in flames from head to toe."

I was fortunate enough to interview two different people who witnessed Charles Moore's self-immolation, Mallie Munn and Buddy Lambert, and have chatted with a couple of other witnesses informally. All of them have a vivid clarity about what they saw Moore doing leading up to his death, and then everything went into slow motion for them, reminiscent of what David Halberstam wrote in witnessing Thich Quang Duc's death in 1963, at a street corner in Saigon. Duc famously self-immolated to protest the Vietnamese regime's oppressive control over Buddhism. Halberstam declared:

> I was to see that sight again, but once was enough. Flames were coming from a human being; his body was slowly withering and shriveling up, his head blackening and charring. In the air was the smell of burning flesh; human beings burn surprisingly quickly. Behind me I could hear the sobbing of the Vietnamese who were now gathering. I was too shocked to cry, too confused to take notes or ask questions, too bewildered even to think.
>
> . . . As he burned he never moved a muscle, never uttered a sound, his outward composure in sharp contrast to the wailing people around him. (128)

Lambert was one of the first two men to run up to Moore and attempt to save his life. He is a man of small stature, covered in faded tattoos and wearing a white tank top when I interviewed him in the summer of 2016. He was an unprepossessing interviewee, and when he first sat down to shoot our interview, I was afraid he wouldn't have much to tell us because he was extremely quiet and nervous. I should never have judged him, though, because he provided more detail than I could have expected.

A warning for readers: Lambert's descriptions in this account are graphic and stress-inducing. He described the sight itself (something I cannot include because the original interview made me sick at my stomach and goes beyond the scope of what I am attempting to accomplish here). For weeks and months afterward, he also vividly recalled the smell of Moore burning, haunting him at times. He would wake up in the middle of the night with that scent entrenched in his memory, and every time he traveled past the parking lot he would be drawn back into these memories.

For those who witnessed Moore's death, they can never erase it. It stays with them.

Not everyone in Grand Saline distinctly remembers Moore's self-immolation and death, however. I spoke with multiple friends and interviewed various people following his death—anywhere between a year and three years later—and though many could name that Moore died and his reasons for dying, they said that people they knew often couldn't. Actually, one of the first people I interviewed, Sasha Mann, a white woman in my graduating class, stated when asked if she knew why Moore died, "He did it because he was a racist, right? He was a part of the KKK?" She had heard the first rumor about Moore and never learned anything else. Others stated that they would often chat with friends and family about Moore's death and some would say he was just crazy and dismiss it and many still did not know that it had occurred at all.

How can a community of three thousand people have such an extreme protest death take place in the center of town, with multiple witnesses and a letter spelling out the exigency that drove the protester, and not have everyone in the community know of the incident and also know of Moore's clearly explained motives?

I first heard about Moore's death around 5:30 p.m. on June 23. I was in my bedroom, reading for my comprehensive exams for my doctoral degree at Texas Christian University. I logged onto Facebook and saw a couple of old Grand Saline friends puzzle over the same question: "Was someone on fire at the Bear Grounds parking lot?" (Bear Grounds is an old nickname for this space.) I kept looking around to better understand what was happening but couldn't find anything. Eventually, later that evening, another Facebook friend messaged me and claimed that he heard that a man had self-immolated in this parking lot because he felt guilty for being part of the KKK in the past.

I was stunned that someone would do this in my hometown, but I was also a bit taken aback by how much this related to my research. I was finishing my comprehensive exams, which focused on race and protest rhetorics, and was working on a dissertation on global protest images and nondiscursive language. I was interested in famous photos of "Tankman" in Tiananmen Square, Black Power at the Olympics, and . . . Thich Quang Duc's self-immolation in Saigon. My dissertation would have more than likely involved analyzing self-immolation, and then a self-immolation actually occurred in my hometown because someone wanted to repent for being in a racist organization. It united my research on race and activism. I was obsessed.

More important, this felt personal. I had been blogging about my racial experiences in Grand Saline for a few years, but no one in Grand Saline was ever interested in my thoughts or wanted to start a conversation. Maybe this extreme mode of death could lead to actual change.

June 23 was a Monday. By Wednesday, June 25, Moore's death had still made no local or regional headlines. I didn't even know his name yet. Why wasn't this making regional or local news? It had the potential to be a state or national story, so it was easily something that should appear in nearby papers. I looked at the *Grand Saline Sun* Facebook page and website. Nothing. I moved to other towns' papers and the county's paper. Still nothing. Finally, I messaged the editor of the *Sun*, Wendi Callaway, because I had a connection with her: I had worked at the *Sun* for one year in 2010, during the first year of my master's work, before I quit to start teaching full-time.

I typed out a message on Facebook: "Hi Wendi, I hope you are doing well! I am reaching out because I have heard a wild story about the man who burned at the Bear Grounds. I heard there's a letter. Do you mind sharing it?"

I waited, watching the " . . . " of her typing out a reply. I was anxious.

"It's not what everyone thinks it is. That wasn't his real reason for doing it," she replied.

Before I could respond, she stated, "I don't want you to scoop me lol."

I explained how I wasn't in the journalism business anymore and only wanted to know the truth—why he died and why people weren't reporting it.

She assured me that there would be a story about it in the weekly issue of the *Sun*, which came out on Thursdays, and said she would send me the letter so I could read it for myself. She also stated that she had heard rumors of local agencies attempting to cover up the incident because they didn't want Grand Saline making national news for racism again, so I promised not to share the letter with anyone.

A few minutes later I read a copy of Moore's letter and finally understood that he was not an ex-member of the KKK; rather, he was an antiracist attempting to change the town. In many ways, I was more fascinated by this perspective. He was a white man who grew up in Grand Saline and believed nothing had changed over the years and wanted to push for more inclusivity. I found his letter inspiring and hopeful and looked forward to seeing what Callaway had to say about Moore in the paper the next day.

I texted my grandma the next morning and asked if she wouldn't mind picking up a copy of the paper. She lived a few miles north and would have to make a twenty-minute drive to get a copy, but she loves nothing more than to be helpful, and she jumped at the opportunity. She would call me later in the afternoon after she went to town.

My phone rang around four. I answered and my grandma quickly exclaimed, "The story's not here!"

"What? That can't be true."

"I'm staring at the front page and it ain't there."

Callaway chose not to put the story at the top of the first page. Instead, she placed it at the bottom of the first page, under the fold—after a story about the school board. Her brief account didn't name Charles Moore and didn't detail the letter that had clearly stated his motivations. Moore made direct claims about the town's racism. He said that he sensed that "most Grand Saline residents just don't want Black people among them" and that the town needs to "open its heart and its doors to Black people, as a sign of the rejection of past sins." In closing his letter, he bluntly claims that he self-immolated to help people move past their prejudices.

None of this made it into Callaway's article.

Instead, she opted not to name Moore and not to detail his letter. She only stated that he committed the self-immolation because of "how things used to be around here." This one phrase told me everything that I needed to know about why she had buried Moore's story. I was furious.

Days went by and no other news came out about Moore.

My grandfather, a Southern Baptist preacher, was retiring from a church and becoming pastor emeritus, so I drove two hours east, just north of Grand Saline, the following weekend to join the celebration of his retirement. My grandfather's final sermon in this small church of a hundred people was, as it always was, centered on love. He stood behind the pulpit one final time with tears in his eyes, arms crossed, thanking his parishioners for the affection they had provided him for the years, and the congregation stood, clapping, applauding him for his service.

I couldn't help comparing my grandfather to Moore. They were around the same age and both practiced what they preached. Moore was just more of an activist than my grandfather. But where was the love for Moore? Where was his recognition? Any acknowledgment? Anything?

Back at home, after eating the lunch buffet that was customary after church, I stood in the kitchen and read the newspaper my grandmother had bought me. I was torn between the love that my grandfather had just preached and the anger that Moore's death had been silenced. I shared my frustration with my mom, grandma, and grandfather, though they didn't fully understand why I was so fascinated with Moore's death. He was just different from them.

"You know, anger can be righteous," my grandfather jumped in while pouring a glass of water. "What made Jesus overturn the money changers' tables in the Gospels? It wasn't him being nice. . . . You can use anger for good."

I always trusted my grandfather's advice. He was the one I connected with most, especially on an intellectual level, so he motivated me to think of ways I could use this anger for change. How could I help? By the time I arrived home Sunday evening I had set out a plan: I emailed ten news organizations on the local and regional level (some in the Dallas–Fort Worth area, some in the Tyler area [the nearest "big" city], and some in Grand Saline's county) with links to the first story, my perspective, and the reasons that I believed it should be covered. I emailed them all Sunday night and went to bed satisfied.

The next day I received a reply.

Kenneth Dean, an investigative reporter with the *Tyler Morning Telegraph*, the largest regional paper in East Texas, emailed me back and wanted to chat about the story. He called that afternoon and we conversed for about an hour as I paced back and forth in my backyard in the Texas summer heat. He asked about my experiences in Grand Saline and my research on race, and a sense of unease crept inside me. This article would attach my name to antiracism in Grand Saline, and I felt anxious because I still had plenty of people I loved who are a part of the community who would be upset with me.

However, I had to do what I thought was right.

The next day Dean published his article online, titled "Madman or Martyr? Retired Minister Sets Self on Fire, Dies," and it was also the front-page story for the *Telegraph*. Though sensationalist in nature (this was more than a false binary question), the article dove into the historical racism and racial makeup of the town and would,

I hoped, start a dialogue about racism there. My hour-long interview boiled down to a few sentences in the piece: "When someone sets themselves on fire in order to commit suicide, they have something to say." And a quotation from me ended the article: "We all want to think that there is no racism among us today and that there isn't any racism on an individual level, but our past memories can affect us as a community. . . . Everyone in Grand Saline knows there is a history, but no one wants to talk about it."

I hoped that the leading story in a major regional paper would force people in Grand Saline to react, especially because of the startling way in which Moore chose to die, publicly.

It didn't.

However, Callaway eventually changed tune in not wanting to talk about race in town. In early July, she published an op-ed (which has now been deleted) on the *Sun* Facebook page that denounced the town's racism but didn't substantially cite evidence to make her claims (some claims can be proven with a cursory glance at research but citations weren't added to the op-ed). She stated in the article, titled "Protesting Racism," that "African Americans were tortured, hung from trees, hung from the Poletown bridge [sic], decapitated and their heads placed on poles in Poletown, burned alive, and God only knows what else." She claimed that Moore didn't do enough to change the situation in town because he was "fearful" of the town's response, and she asked for the community to actually recognize their history.

This left her open to criticism and, tangentially, allowed for the gatekeepers in Grand Saline to act swiftly. In a letter to the editor on July 17, 2014, titled "Racism in Grand Saline? The Historical Truths," thirteen citizens signed a letter claiming to offer the "historically proven facts" about racism in the community. The letter was signed by local dentist and former president of the Chamber of Commerce Dr. James B. Lea; storeowner Galloway Darby; Mary Jane Smith Hollowell, whose family had owned the City Food Store; local insurance agent Harry Clifford; high school English teacher Emily Clifford Pugh, whose family had owned Pugh Hardware; and a few other local business owners and prominent citizens.

The letter essentially called Callaway a liar and said there is nothing particularly interesting about the racism in Grand Saline. Their response was taken as the be-all-and-end-all for the conversation. Many townsfolk shared it on social media because they believed it to be their best version of the truth (or a version of the "truth" that corresponds with their ideologies)—published by outstanding citizens. I was furious because though some of the evidence they presented was true, many of their claims were half-truths that were accepted just because of their reputations.

By the end of the summer, Callaway was no longer editor of the newspaper.

The *Tyler Morning Telegraph* published another story on Moore on July 2, titled "Stepson-in-Law of Man Who Set Self on Fire in Grand Saline: Final Act Was 'Ultimate Sacrifice,'" that included the views of Moore's stepson-in-law and good friend and further attempted to parse his motives for dying. Another week and a half would pass before Moore's story ended up in the *Dallas Morning News*. Melissa Repko, the author, attempted to better contextualize Moore's death and make his actions seem more nuanced and less sensational. He sounded like an actual human being in her words. A few days later an article showed up in the *Washington Post* that was just a summary of all the other articles written by that point. Finally, in December 2014, six months after Moore's death, Michael Hall published his long-read article on Moore's life and death in *Texas Monthly*. It was an eloquently written account of Moore's life and continuous struggle to advocate for people—chronicling his early years in Grand Saline and his various protests.

That was it.

Moore's death would go down in obscurity, with more questions than answers, and without any public dialogue about racism in Grand Saline.

In the fall of 2014, my dissertation chair, Brad Lucas, convinced me to turn my entire dissertation into rhetorical analyses of Moore's death and self-immolation on a global scale. I would carry the torch, but no one reads dissertations (do committees, even, really?). Maybe that would be the end of Moore's story in the public sphere.

Fate had a different idea, though.

Over a year later, on September 2, 2015, two of my friends, Kate Keenan (a friend from graduate school) and Joshua David Keenan, decided that they wanted to create a small makeshift memorial in the parking lot where Moore died to honor his legacy (see Figure 5). Joshua grew up in Canton, twelve miles south of Grand Saline, and the two of them were visiting family before they decided to venture to Grand Saline and honor Moore.

The sign reads "R.I.P. Charles R. Moore" and was held up by zip ties around a yellow pole, only a few feet away from where Moore had burned fifteen months earlier. They placed a beautiful bouquet of flowers above the sign. To my knowledge, this was the first public memorial dedicated to Moore's life and death. No other public artifact in Grand Saline mentions his name. The Keenans told me in a joint interview that they felt obligated to honor him because they were so moved by his death. Though they weren't from Grand Saline, they connected with Moore and his perceived act of sacrifice.

Figure 5. A small, makeshift memorial created to honor Moore's death.

They needed to create a gesture—even if small—in remembrance of him, so they fashioned this sign and bought the flowers.

The Keenans sent me the images of this memorial a few minutes after they created it. I was in the midst of writing my dissertation and felt no love from people in my hometown. Though I knew some friends who were empathetic with Moore and his immolation, most of the chatter around him revolved around discourses of "craziness" (and thus ableism). Still, two of my friends who lived an hour away from town had journeyed to the place where Moore died because they felt compelled to engage with his story. The obvious love they held toward Moore and his protest was a driving force for me, fueling me during the dissertation slog. Just knowing that others cared about Moore's legacy motivated me to keep writing.

Though the memorial was small and unassuming, I wondered how long it would remain intact. It did not obscure any parking spaces and was not offensive in the least. Would people in Grand Saline let it stand? I spoke with a friend in the community, Sandy Packer, about the incident and questioned its legitimacy for townsfolk. Would the sign exist for a few months? Maybe one month? Maybe just a couple of weeks? Three days after the Keenans fashioned the memorial, I asked Packer to keep track of it, so I could know when it was destroyed.

She messaged me after returning from town on the same day: "It's already gone."

I knew it wouldn't last very long, but I was surprised that it took at most three days—perhaps less—for someone (if not a few people) in the community to destroy it. I couldn't imagine the memorial being abolished that quickly. This act reinforced the town's secretive nature. They didn't want to deal with this memory; they want to move past it, to erase it.

Would *anything* make them remember or force them to confront their stories?

One afternoon a couple of months later, in November 2015, I exited my office at TCU to head home and crossed paths with a friend and lecturer in the English department, Kristen Lacefield. She told me that she had a director friend in Austin who produces phenomenal cultural documentaries, and he was looking for his next project. Kristen enthusiastically explained to him my dissertation work, and he was interested in potentially making a film from my story.

"Do you want me to get his info so y'all can chat about it?" she asked in the parking lot as I was getting into my car.

I had always imagined this as a film but wanted to do it myself. So I initially told her no, until that evening, when I realized I had no idea how to make a film.

I finally reached out to Joel Fendelman, the director, and we talked on the phone on a Thursday morning in late November while I sat in a coffee shop. I told him all the ins and outs of Moore's death, the racism in Grand Saline, the public conversation, people I had interviewed, and stories on this subject. He expressed interest but was still weighing some other options, yet once he heard the idea it possessed him as it had me. By March 2016, we partnered to make the film, and he asked me to be the lead producer on the project. (Great, what does a producer do?) I would lead the scouting trip, find people to interview, conduct preinterviews and film interviews, and help in narrative formation.

In May 2016 we set out on our first scouting trip, which would open the door to shooting the film throughout the summer and into the early fall. For documentaries, scouting trips are developmental procedures that film teams use to find potential characters and sense a film's aesthetic. Joel had some of his own funds tied into the film and a few grants from the University of Texas at Austin, where the film would be his master's thesis. Yet Joel was no amateur in filmmaking. He had directed and produced multiple feature films and documentaries and screened at the Montreal World Film Festival, Brooklyn Film Festival, Tribeca Film Festival, and the SXSW (South by Southwest) Film Festival. He knew what he was doing.

Though we chatted on the phone a few times throughout the winter and spring, we never met in person until the night before our scouting trip.

Joel arrived at the house that I shared with a few graduate student roommates on a Thursday evening, and I was overwhelmed with his generosity and spirit. Though he was obviously a skilled director and filmmaker, his heartwarming and down-to-earth demeanor propelled our friendship. He never made me feel stupid for not understanding how filmmaking works, and his presence always invited me to learn. We bonded over our love of storytelling and quickly developed a unique good-cop (Joel) and bad-cop (me) relationship that came about naturally while interviewing people. It was clear we would be a good team, and most important, friends, for the rest of our lives.

The next day we drove to Grand Saline and interviewed people, without a camera, and scouted locations that might be featured in the film. We chatted with local newspaper editor B. R. Fite; local historian Elvis Allen; and local antique shop owner Chet Yant. Though they all discredited and downplayed the racism, it was clear they had a lot to say about Moore and the town's legacy. Their characters would shine if we placed a camera in front of them.

Going into this project, I imagined we would get a fair amount of pushback from people who didn't want us "race-baiting," but I was pleasantly surprised. Many of the elders in the community welcomed our interviews after we got in with the first few older men. Once we interviewed the local historian, the editor of the newspaper, and the preacher for the largest church in town, finding interviewees became easy. Our main tactic for securing interviews turned to "Well, last week we interviewed the town historian, and he said . . . " We constructed our ethos in the town simply by listing all those we had already interviewed. That worked for some of the older men (and though we asked many older women in town to be interviewed, they often responded with some version of, "Oh, I don't know anything about that. You should talk to my husband," which was frustrating) but not for the younger folk.

Only five younger people (two men and three women between the ages of eighteen and thirty-three) appear in the film or allowed us to interview them, and they were the more liberal, antiracist people from the community. We reached out to at least twenty or twenty-five folks in that age range to see if they would do interviews. Most of them told me no because I was in the middle of that age bracket, and all of them knew of me as a "race baiter" who would be doing a hit piece on the town. So most people didn't want to talk.

However, a few people wanted to be interviewed but couldn't.

Early in the filming process I reached out to Sandy Packer, the person who had informed me that the memorial was destroyed. I always trust her takes on issues in the community and knew she would be an unmitigated force in the film—when she speaks, you listen. She is always honest with me, and I never imagined that she wouldn't want to go in front of the camera.

"I can't do it," she responded to me after I sent her a message on a social media app. "I can't do it because my family lives here, my kids go to school here. We can't move, and I don't want to be ousted from the town." Her response made sense, yet I didn't see it coming because I never imagined the consequences of being in the film while living in Grand Saline. I had the status of an insider—growing up in Grand Saline, having lots of friends still in the area, and having many elders in the community know my grandparents—but the *safety* of an outsider—I didn't have to be in the community unless I wanted to be there (my mother had moved a few miles away from the town once I graduated). For people like Packer, speaking has consequences, and Callaway's departure as the editor of the newspaper was evidence of what could take place.

Packer also recited a story from the 1990s when some teenagers spoke out about the town's racism and were ridiculed by the town. Three students in a journalism class wanted to investigate various stories they had heard about the KKK meeting at Clark's Ferry. As Packer puts it, "The boys were immediately shut down by people in town, especially the old men at the coffee shop." She claims that the three students were told not to look into the incident and that they felt deflated by the pushback of townsfolk.

This incident became a major talking point within the community. Historian Elvis Allen states that "renewed interest" about Grand Saline's history of racism occurred because these boys were doing this research and were "getting a lot of the facts wrong." He contends that he doesn't have a problem with the students doing the research but rather just being erroneous in their claims (i.e., they should state only his position on the matter). Other residents remember hearing stories about what happened to these students when they asked people to discuss Clark's Ferry. They remember narratives of students trying to "cause trouble" (Amanda Jones) or students barred from investigating Clark's Ferry (Emily Erwin). Nonetheless, many residents in the area recall that the students who looked into this issue got into trouble and were asked not to investigate it. It wouldn't be too much of a leap to see how residents might misinterpret local community members being upset with the students getting their history wrong instead of being upset with them for investigating the incident, but, in truth, that doesn't matter, because the *perception* of what took place is that residents in the area demanded the high schoolers stop doing their research.

This incident still felt raw for some people in the community who remembered it, and it was cited a couple of times as to why people didn't want to be interviewed by us.

We finished most of the production uneventfully through the summer of 2016, completing five different shoots in town with varying success. We returned one final time in September to capture images of the homecoming parade. In Grand Saline—as in many similar communities around the United States—homecoming is a big annual event where alumni return to town to watch a varsity football game. Homecoming festivals culminated each year with the annual bonfire on Thursday night, a huge woodpile built on the school grounds in which players, residents, and alumni would gather around as they made speeches about their victory against Friday's opponent and burn effigies of that opponent (sometimes a jersey or sometimes a wooden version of their mascot).

This image of people watching a massive bonfire right outside of the school would be a perfect symbol we could juxtapose with Moore's death, but we needed permission to film on school grounds.

I knew that the superintendent of the school wouldn't accept our presence if we said that this film was about the self-immolation that had occurred in town, so I turned to a more vague approach. I introduced myself as a graduate student and a former resident of Grand Saline and said we were doing a film on the town and had been filming throughout the summer. I asked if we could film the homecoming parade and football game because those encapsulate the traditions of Grand Saline so well. I felt bad for not telling the whole truth, but I knew there was no other way around this.[1]

The superintendent agreed to our terms via email and in a voicemail.

We arrived that Thursday night at the bonfire west of the school, and the nerves overcame me. I knew the eyes would be on us tonight, and in some ways that forced me to work through my relationship with the town. It was already dusk when we arrived and the cars littered the open pasture. I hoped that maybe we could get lost in the crowd, but I also knew I was in charge if people started asking questions.

Joel put his camera on a Steadicam—a camera stabilizer that allows you to walk and capture footage smoothly, without bumpiness—and our soundperson went to capture the ambiance of the crowd. I saw an old high school friend and went over to nervously chat. As soon as we shook hands, I sensed that he was uncomfortable being near me. Maybe we weren't that close anymore . . . or maybe he knew the perception of being associated with me, so I stepped away and tried to keep to myself. The eyes were on me.

After thirty minutes or so, the principal of the school came over and asked what we were doing. He was the older brother of Marcus, my best friend from ten years earlier. We chatted like old friends for a bit (I felt more relaxed around him), and I showed him the email from the superintendent giving us permission. He jumped on the phone with the superintendent and chatted for a bit, and by the time he wrapped up the call we were already finished filming.

"Watch out," he told me. "The superintendent seems misinformed about what this is about."

He was right, of course.

The next day I received a call from the superintendent, and he chewed me out for a good ten minutes for not telling him the full story. I felt guilty, I really did, but I hoped that the footage we captured was for the greater good. He asked me to delete it. Legally, we had no obligation to delete the footage, but did we have a moral one? The guilt tore at me.

(The final scene of *Man on Fire* is an image of the bonfire.)

During our final night in town, after filming the bonfire and feeling further shunned by the superintendent, we ate at a local restaurant, and could finally breathe because the hard part was over. We had captured the homecoming parade and interviewed everyone we needed from the town. It was perhaps our most successful shoot.

Our waitress, a young woman in her twenties who constantly seemed in a hurry, brought over waters for the crew, and we ordered our food. After we finished ordering I turned back to Joel to chat.

"What you did the other night was wrong," the waitress stated matter-of-factly, still staring at me.

"Excuse me?"

"You have no right to film children without the permission of an adult."

Joel and I had had multiple conversations about this, so I had recently learned the ins and outs of filming people in large events. I shared my thoughts with her, but she didn't care about my position. She smiled at us and walked away.

"Do you think she's going to spit on my burger?" I jokingly asked the table.

"Probably," Joel retorted.

I ate it anyway.

Through the fall and winter, Joel edited the film into different cuts, and we focused on narrative sequencing. We ultimately decided on what we thought would work best—interviews about Moore, his life and death, and racism in Grand Saline that would be dispersed between a retelling of Moore's final day and self-immolation. We filmed reenactment scenes one long weekend in February 2017 with an actor who looked surprisingly like Moore and went through the minutiae of his final day—Moore dressing, driving his car, sitting in the parking lot, and eventually self-immolating (from a tasteful and restrained perspective).

By May 2017 the film was complete, and we submitted it to film festivals and various programs. I also graduated from TCU and had secured a tenure-track job at Middlebury College. Though some of the work felt complete (aside from this book), we had yet to receive external feedback outside of Joel's thesis committee (they loved the film).

In October, we received terrific news: Slamdance Film Festival, the loveable stepchild of Sundance in Park City, Utah, had accepted *Man on Fire* for its world premiere, and *Independent Lens* had picked up our film for their 2018–2019 season on PBS (though we were sworn to secrecy until July 2018)! We learned both of these pieces of news within a week of each other, and I felt so . . . heard, for once. Though Moore's story hadn't made the national news his death deserved three years earlier, maybe our film would honor him properly. Our hard work was paying off.

Man on Fire successfully toured through the spring of 2018—winning an International Documentary Association award and airing at multiple film festivals, and we were interviewed by many different publications about our film and Moore's story. Yet we also had a unique opportunity to screen our film in a beautiful old theater in Tyler, Texas, right down the road from Grand Saline. Paul Streufert, Director of the Honors College at the University of Texas at Tyler, my undergraduate institution, thought this could be a great conversation piece for honors students and wanted to open it for the public. Joel and I invited everyone interviewed in the film to attend and publicized the event with local newspapers and news stations.

One of the first publicity emails I sent went to an editor of a newspaper in a town near Grand Saline. I wrote about the film and what we were trying to accomplish with a public screening, asking nearby residents to attend. At the end of the email, I stated, clearly,

"We are also attempting to recruit members of Grand Saline to attend the event so we can have an open dialogue about race and racism in the community."

The editor replied to the email the next day that she remembered Moore's death and couldn't attend the event (though I was only asking her to promote it for her local audience). However, she did want to know "if any aspect of the man's potential mental illness was examined," which corresponds with the local narratives dismissing Moore that I heard from the very beginning of my research process. She continued:

> One of my co-workers grew up in the town. She raised children there who were very active in the schools and local youth league sports. Her son played with a Black young man from [a nearby town], the son of a well-liked well-known family from here. The boys and families had known each other for a while and she viewed them as friends. One day the father from [the nearby town], a Black man, learned she was from Grand Saline. He expressed his shock, incredulous that she was from Grand Saline because she and her family were good people and not racists. She felt she had been viewed in the same manner as someone who experiences racism. So please be aware of the danger of painting an entire town of people with a broad brush. (Personal email)

Why did she assume we would essentialize this community and not be nuanced in our response? Why be defensive instead of just asking me about my intent? Her response angered me because it assumed I was using a "broad brush" in painting the town. She *assumed* that I had *assumed* that the entire town is racist. It's not just that she didn't promote the film (which would have been fine), but that she felt she needed to lecture me about the *real* racial issues in the area and that being charged as racist is equivalent to actual racism.

Even though I was proud of the work Joel and I accomplished, it felt as though we would never break through to East Texas. Though the film isn't for them per se, they were the ones I always wanted to reach.

Joel and I flew to Tyler in late February 2018 for our screening on a Wednesday. We successfully promoted the film with a couple of news station interviews outside the theater and appeared on the front page of the *Tyler Morning Telegraph* the next day (Cory Mc-Coy, "Filmmakers Hope Movie Fosters Conversation about Racial Divide"), the same paper that had featured Moore on their front page almost four years earlier.

Streufert brought well over 150 honors students to attend the film, and we packed out the theater with almost 250 people in attendance. Though I had attended some film festivals and responded to Q&As there, this felt different. There were multiple interviewees in attendance and at least a handful of Grand Saline residents. Also, my family packed out an entire row of seats at the back of the theater (customary for back-row Christians). I had never felt the weight of the film before, the idea that we could potentially have an impact on people's lives—be it people from my hometown, or people who knew Moore, or someone maybe challenging their own notions of racism. Yet here we were, showing off our creation to a large East Texas audience.

After the screening Joel and I took the stage ready to answer any questions, and a line formed near the microphone. Was anyone going to challenge us?

Some of the questions were on the production side of the film ("How did you film the self-immolation?" or "How did you find the people you interviewed?"), but many of them went into larger issues of racism ("Has Grand Saline changed?" or "Would you say the entire town is racist?"). I was happy that we were able to engage with locals about the complexity of these issues, not just focusing on how the film was made but what the film means to people in the audience.

After chatting with students and a few other audience members once the Q&A finished, I went in search of my family. Maybe it was the familiar post–football game routine or maybe it was because of how much I respected his opinion, but I knew I needed to talk to my grandfather.

He had changed since my high school days. His 6'5" frame now slumped forward, and he had lost fifty or sixty pounds due to being on dialysis. He never traveled too far anymore (dialysis three times a week) and was always tired by the early evening, yet he told me there was no way he was going to miss the screening. I could never escape his love.

I recalled talking with my grandfather years earlier about this project—right after Moore died—and how he helped guide me through my righteous indignation. Even in guiding me, he didn't fully understand why I was interested in Moore, but he helped nonetheless.

When I found him, he opened his arms—wider than most humans can reach—and engulfed me in his love and spirit.

"I get it now," he whispered to me. "I get it."

It's my most precious memory of him.

6

Silenced

> Are there racists in Grand Saline today? No doubt. Are we a
> racist community? God forbid. As business owners and citizens
> of Grand Saline we regret and resent the stigma that has been
> perpetuated concerning our community.
> —"Racism in Grand Saline? The Historical Truths"

WENDI CALLAWAY, FORMER editor of the *Grand Saline Sun*, was the
one who first told me the correct story about Moore's death. I had
heard a few rumors, but once she sent me his letter and chatted
with me, I fully understood Moore's claimed reasons for dying.
Callaway was completely honest with me in our one-on-one cor-
respondence. So I was very much shocked when she chose not to
make the story of Moore the leading headline in the newspaper
(she placed it under the fold) and only referred to Moore dying for
"how things used to be around here." Though I was clearly upset
with her actions, her framing illustrated the way racial discussions
begin—and end—in Grand Saline.

This one phrase relayed vital information to readers of the paper. For outsiders who knew nothing about Grand Saline's history of racism, this sentence didn't say much. "How things used to
be" could refer to many different historical moments and might
not even be related to Grand Saline's particular history. Outsiders
could easily brush past it. Insiders, though, knew *exactly* what this
meant—Grand Saline's history of racism has existed for well over
a century, and everyone in town knows of it (even if they disagree
with its veracity). Callaway didn't need to name racism for everyone
in town to know that racism was at the heart of Moore's death. Arguably, she rhetorically framed this story around *silence* to absolve

herself of blame. If she named Moore and his motivations, the people of the town would chastise her and say that she was stirring up racial discord. This isn't just me speculating. A week after the article came out, Callaway published an editorial on the *Sun* Facebook page[1] in which she named racism as a problem in the community.

She was fired from her job three months later, according to journalist Daniel Villarreal. When Villarreal asked the publisher, Dan Moore, why he fired her, Moore responded: "It was time for a change."

There are various types of silences and silencing apparent in the *Sun* article, as they represent synecdoches of the larger system of white supremacist silencing that exists in Grand Saline. In some sense, Callaway's silence represents a form of repression. If she were to be vocal about Moore's death and the racism in the community, residents who are sensitive about their history of racism might chastise her and call for her job (as they seemingly did a few weeks later after she wrote her editorial). She, like all residents of Grand Saline, understands the power of naming racism and understands that any claims of bigotry will be met with hardline defenses by people in town. So this silence could be perceived as an internalized mechanism of survival, one that she utilizes because she knows her livelihood might be affected if she names racism. It might not even be a conscious act.

Similarly, her silence in this situation might be perceived as an act of power, a textual wink to her audience that she understands the racial situation that underpins Moore's story but that she does not have to explicitly acknowledge racism for her audience to understand it. Textual winks are rhetorical tactics that may not look like much on the surface yet "speak implicitly about a discourse and still claim allegiance to a cause without employing overt language" (Sanchez, "Trump"). Charles E. Morris III sees these winks as promoting "an ideology of difference" because they seemingly say one thing but imply something else to a particular audience (230). Callaway's claim that Moore died for "how things used to be around here" is a textual wink that doesn't explicitly say much but says to people in Grand Saline that Moore died in a protest against racism. Only the insiders in the community would understand this wink. Employing a wink could be perceived as an act of power in silencing. It affords the rhetor the space to claim insider status by invoking language that only insiders would know. Simply by employing a wink the rhetor claims some authority via knowledge of an audience.

However, the *Grand Saline Sun*'s coverage of Moore's death is not the sole act of silencing, regarding racism or Moore's death, that has occurred within the community. This chapter—along with the narrative from the previous chapter—argues that silencing is another, final rhetorical act of preservation that Grand Saline uses primarily to challenge dissenters and maintain white supremacy. People attempted to silence Moore's protest act from the public discourse (and erase his death); they also attempted to silence me during the making and promotion of *Man on Fire*.

SILENCING AS SUSTAINING

In her robust analysis of this subject in *Unspoken: A Rhetoric of Silence*, Cheryl Glenn says, poetically,

> Employed as a tactical strategy or inhabited in deference to authority, silence resonates loudly along the corridors of purposeful language use, of rhetoric. Whether choice or im/position, silence can reveal positive or negative abilities, fulfilling or withholding traits, harmony or disharmony, success or failure. Just like speech, silence can deploy power; it can defer to power. It all depends. (15)

To Glenn, silence, which is often perceived to be a negation of rhetoric, can be rhetorical and does carry many different meanings. Silence doesn't always have to involve an actor giving up power in a particular situation; silence can be an act of power. Thus, while we often think of silence in terms of someone being silenced—such as the discourse surrounding #MeToo victims (Prasad)—silence can also empower people. For instance, every time a professor asks a question in the classroom and basks in the silence, waiting for a student to answer, they rely upon the authoritative power of silence to persuade someone to speak.

Glenn's work on silencing is pivotal in understanding ways that people *use* and *disuse* discursive language. Glenn states, "We live inside the act of discourse, to be sure, but we cannot assume that a *verbal* matrix is the only one in which the articulations and conduct of the mind take place—regardless of the measure of inward or outward persuasion" (153) and then quotes José Ortega y Gasset: "People leave some things unsaid in *order* to be able to say others" (246). She argues that sometimes not saying anything says more than verbal language would. For instance, as a popular-culture trope, when someone in a movie tells someone that they love them and the person doesn't respond or hesitates to speak, we inherently know that silence speaks volumes. It tells the audience that the individual doesn't feel the same way. The crux of Glenn's text is to demonstrate the various types of silences (especially in feminist discourse) and build a rhetorical theory of silencing.

However, some scholars, such as Cynthia Ryan, have critiqued Glenn not upon the basis of silence as a rhetorical tactic but because the implications of this research can be unwieldy. Ryan, in responding to Glenn's first essay on silencing in *JAC*, writes, "I think it is risky to teach silence as a rhetorical strategy before we have fleshed out the complexity of this art and the multiple and often contradictory ways in which it might be interpreted in private and public contexts. Gestures of silence, as Glenn has acknowledged, are filled with unquiet implications. We must carefully and responsibly examine what lies beneath" (676). She reasons that though the impact of Glenn's research is obvious, we need to better understand the ramifications of silencing—how it affects people, how to use it properly, and how to teach it—before we fully integrate it into the field. Ryan bases her argument upon the weight of silencing; she views it as a powerful rhetorical tool that needs to be fully developed before the field starts integrating it into all facets of our work and teaching.

Other scholars discuss silence in specific rhetorical situations, illustrating that silencing can affect issues of identity, legality, and pedagogy. J. Logan Smilges, for instance, focuses on silencing as it relates to the "queer body" and "the particular significations and stigmatizations that often accompany queerness" on the dating app Grindr (80). They focus on "rhetorical quieting," or the "self-regulation" that queer people often use as a means of navigating spaces. Shelby P. Bell focuses on silence in the legal realm, investigating silence as it relates to the *Berghuis v. Thompkins* court case, which revolved around Van Chester Thompkins's "admitting" to murder after being quiet for two hours and forty-five minutes during a police interrogation and questioned whether his persistent maintaining of silence required the interrogation to end in accordance with the law (177). Bell highlights the risks of using silence as a rhetorical tool when people who are marginalized attempt to utilize it as an act of power. Byron Hawk takes silence back to the traditions of rhetoric, referring to it as creating the possibility of listening and labeling it as "the source of invention" (384). All of these examples illustrate the ways silence can be used for rhetorical purposes—sometimes employed from a position of power and sometimes forced upon a person. My analysis emphasizes these conversations as they relate to white supremacy, suggesting specifically that agents for white supremacy in Grand Saline employ methods of silencing to quiet detractors of the town's racist culture.

Silencing of racial dissenters in Grand Saline exists as a form of control. The community acts as a homogenous collective when issues of race come out in public. If a person in the community were to critique the town's racism, as Callaway did in 2014, they would be publicly rejected for their opposition, as Callaway was. In this way, the community uses silencing as an act of preservation—a way to keep their community intact and defend against those who attack them. It preserves the community by creating a unified front that makes any dissenter seem alone in their stance. No rifts arise during these moments; dissenters are simply painted as a small minority who have no legitimacy facing off against the culture's hegemonic view of race. The silencing makes the dissenter feel alone, feel abandoned, feel treated as untrustworthy.

Silencing encompasses a network of gestures and frames—including silencing people, silencing media, erasing narratives, erasing memories, and many more tactics not discussed in this chapter.

These tactics can be used by any person or collective to oppress marginalized people or to demonstrate power. They can fundamentally alter how discourse is discussed or not discussed in a community. While this chapter emphasizes silencing within the white supremacist culture of Grand Saline, it can also be employed in many other situations revolving around issues of gender, sexuality, religion, and other identity markers that mark power structures and constraints.

ERASING CHARLES MOORE

The silencing of the message of Moore's death began soon after he lit himself on fire, yet it's important to note that not all of these silences come from impure motives. Many people, I believe, were doing what they thought was right—and their actions might be right—but that doesn't mean that they still did not effectively silence Moore's protest.

All Grand Saline citizens could easily find the site where Moore perished—the parking lot stripes that he sat upon when he self-immolated retained burn marks. However, only a few days later, those yellow stripes were repainted to fit in with the rest of the parking lot (Munn; Yant). I am unsure who repainted the area, but the decision probably came from the city. It makes sense: Moore's death was a traumatic experience for those who witnessed it. Buddy Lambert, a witness to the incident, stated that he remembers Moore's death every time he enters the parking lot or drives by it. Moore's death scarred him, and that site is a living reminder of that fiery death. As Lambert illustrates, the charred marks on the pavement could easily trigger those who watched Moore burn.

This act of repainting also erases any memory of Moore. Moore wanted his death to create a new conversation about racism in the community and his burn marks were a symbolic reminder of what he did and why he did it. Those marks were reminders of white supremacy and bigotry, and the community decided to simply erase them. About a week after Moore's fiery act, there was no evidence that a protest ever occurred in this space. Had the community left the marks of his death, people would have to confront the reasons he died; they would have been nudged to seek truth. However, erasing the marks from the parking lot provides the community a chance to act as if nothing took place. They don't have to be reminded of the problems in town. They can live their lives without dealing with the effects of Moore's death.

Of course, I think many readers understand the assumed intention behind this erasure. It probably does not come from a place of hatred. This is just a way for Grand Saline to move on from Moore's death and to give those traumatized a sense of peace. The erasure of a makeshift memorial in honor of Moore's life is a different story, though.

I have no idea who took down this memorial, as it is a similar situation to the person who repainted the parking stripes. It could have been someone from the city. It could have been a resident who didn't want people in town to remember Moore in any capacity. It could have been someone who even thought of it as graffiti and threw it away. Nonetheless, the makeshift memorial to Moore is similar to other public artifacts that memorialize public deaths, like roadside crash memorials. Most people feel comfortable driving past roadside crash memorials because though they might bring us pain in remembering our own deceased, we can look at them and see this as a public act of grief (Bednar, "Materialising Memory" and "Killing Memory"). Their rhetorical nature invites us to realize our own mortality, yet we mostly empathize with those who lost someone in seemingly senseless tragedies.

The structure and nature of Moore's memorial isn't much different from those of other roadside crash memorials. It resides in a public space that corresponds with where he died. It simply mentions his name and that he died, without even being overtly political (though, of course, placing the memorial is a political act). It can be interpreted as someone attempting to publicly mourn a man's death. In that sense, there would be no reason to erase it. The memorial isn't making a statement about Moore's politics; it is as apolitical as a public memorial dedicated to Moore's death could be. But someone still destroyed it quickly, possibly because of its perceived politics. While roadside memorials exalt those who died tragically by accident, Moore's memorial honored someone who died for a cause. That within itself might convince some people that he does not deserve a public memorial—his death was too contested. We will probably never truly know the intent behind this erasure, but this act nonetheless erased the memory of Moore's death and the antiracism he championed.

While these two erasures attempted to dissociate Moore from the physical place where he died, the letter from community members in response to Callaway's op-ed went even further to ostracize him and exclude any mention of racism in the community.

The letter quoted in this chapter's epigraph, written by well-known residents in the town, is savvy—positioning these people as the arbiters of the local history of racism. Since their history is "the facts" (which, suspiciously, doesn't name all the facts I will list below), they demonstrate how Callaway was wrong in her op-ed while also illustrating that Moore was misguided in his act of self-immolation. The beginning of the letter states that all of their "facts" are taken from the Freedman's Bureau and local historian Elvis Allen. The letter first discusses the history of Poletown, a community in the area where Black people were supposedly lynched (as stated in Chapters 3 and 4). The group points to the Van Zandt County Historical Commission marker in the area, which says that the name "Pole Town" stemmed from residents building homes in the area from saplings. While this seems plausible, the authors don't mention why the community's name remains uniquely tied to the white doctor who was decapitated for assisting Black people and had his head hung on a pole. This, of course, is why many people associate Poletown with lynchings, because a doctor was literally lynched for helping Black people in the area. Most interesting is their framing of this incident (which, again, they do not tie into the story of the area). They state that a former Confederate soldier, James Ashton, murdered a Black man, Joe Garrett, and a white man, Dr. Page. They continue, "Doctor Page treated the freedmen living in the Jordan's Saline area [Jordan's Saline was a community near Grand Saline that folded at the turn of the twentieth century]. Dr. Page (a Caucasian) was decapitated, his body mutilated and his head" suspended from a tree or hung on a pole (there were contradicting reports). The authors never even illustrate *why* both of these men were killed—outright bigotry. In my interview with Allen, he stated clearly that both men were lynched because Dr. Page would treat Black patients, yet, though the authors claim Allen as a source, they never employ his historical research in their article. The authors couldn't even explicitly note the historical lynchings near the town and never make connections between the story of Poletown and the lynching of Dr. Page and Joe Garrett. The ways these citizens dissociate themselves from issues of racism and rhetorically position themselves establish that they cannot deal with their own substantiated truths publicly.

The letter continues by pointing out that Jordan's Saline had 89 African Americans and 119 Caucasians during the 1870 census. In 1898, with Jordan's Saline dwindling because of the rise of Grand Saline, Grand Saline reportedly had advertisements in regional newspapers claiming that they had "fifteen African-American families and one African-American owned business and would welcome more." The number of Black families in the area diminished during this post-Reconstruction era, and the 2010 census points to fewer than 10 people who identify as Black in Grand Saline. There are no Black families that I know of in town, and most of the Black people in the community are of mixed race. So what happened between the large Black population in 1870 and the minuscule Black population as of 2010?

The letter also distances the community from the Ku Klux Klan, though they admit that the KKK was "indeed active . . . in Van Zandt County and throughout the South" (which, of course, absolves them of agency in Klan activity because it was "everywhere"). The authors cite Allen as saying that the county realized that "no good was coming" from the KKK, so the organization went away in the post-Reconstruction era. (They do correctly note that Callaway misconstrued the histories of the KKK and the Freemasons.) However, this is one of their weakest "facts." They opened the letter saying that everything they listed would be truths proven with evidence, yet *multitudes* of pieces of evidence suggest that the KKK remained in and around Grand Saline for decades. For instance,

Moore claimed that he remembered hearing about the Klan in the 1940s and 1950s when he lived in town. B. R. Fite stated that a Klan rally occurred in the middle of Grand Saline in the 1990s. Chance Sauseda is quoted in a news report stating that he saw the KKK with his own eyes one night while visiting Clark's Ferry in the 1990s (Stewart). Even as recently as 2016, multiple fliers appeared in the Grand Saline area recruiting for the KKK (Sanchez, "Trump"; Colston). Ample historical and contemporary evidence suggests that the Klan not only existed in Grand Saline but still has an active presence there today, but the authors of the letter fail to mention these facts.

The authors, however, do attempt to defend themselves against critique by mentioning a counterpoint to their history, written in a 1909 article from the *Sun* in which the editor of that newspaper wrote that a massacre of Black people had occurred in the town during the post-Reconstruction era and that the bones littered the lake of the salt prairie. The town leaders call the article "preposterous" and without "connection to fact." Allen argues that the article is "tongue-in-cheek" or perhaps a way to sell newspapers (which absolutely could be true, but, as I noted in Chapter 4, I imagine that if an editor were trying to sell papers, they might put this story on the cover, instead of running it at the bottom of page 1). In this way, the letter's authors claim that even the stories of their past racism—stories that have existed for well over a century—have nothing to do with their perception problem today. They quash any credence this article has by having a historian suggest why an editor might write such an article, without actually interrogating why their racism problem has existed for so long in the first place. This makes an implicit argument: anyone who believes that Grand Saline has a racism problem because this perception has existed for so long isn't dealing with "facts" and doesn't have to be taken seriously.

Nonetheless, one of the most egregious parts of the authors' defense—even outside of misconstruing facts or moving past records of the KKK—occurs at the end of their letter, when they misinterpret how lynching history works. After suggesting that racism was only a problem in the period from the 1930s to the 1950s, the authors write:

A simple search through the archives of the Van Zandt County Historical Commission or an inquiry to the Van Zandt County Sherriff's Department, the Texas Department of Public Safety, the Texas Rangers, or even the FBI would have revealed some type of record of illegal activities that occurred in Grand Saline and in Van Zandt County. Had violence, hangings, immolations, or any other murder actually have [sic] happened, these events would have been reported to the authorities and there would have been national coverage of the events just as there was of the tragic and horrible events that occurred in other areas of the South.

This is a direct response to Callaway's unsubstantiated claims, but more important it suggests what these authors think about the era of lynching: *all* lynchings were reported to higher state and national agencies and made national coverage. Of course, this directly contradicts what we know from actual historians. Danny Lewis at the *Smithsonian* claims that "it's unlikely historians will ever know just how many lynchings happened throughout the history of the United States, as many likely went unreported, or were not classified as lynchings in documentation at the time." New scholarship in *Historical Methods* even suggests that the data we have on lynchings is poor because it is often unreported and unrecorded on state levels (Cook 61). Though it may be plausible that if Grand Saline had had multitudes of lynchings there would be historical evidence, it is wrong to propose that the fact that there are no reports in government databases illustrates that there were no lynchings, because such a claim contradicts contemporary historical research. A "simple search" doesn't corroborate anything.

Moreover, the letter writers' claim is once again an effective form of silencing. It tells residents that since historical evidence can't prove that lynchings took place in Grand Saline, the town cannot be described as racist. Of course, doing/not doing lynchings is not the sole criterion for being a racist community. Still, it effectively silences Callaway's op-ed and Moore's act by submitting that both are inconsequential and pointless. Overall, the long-read letter to the editor challenges assumptions about the perception of Grand

Saline and frames a certain "truth" for its audience that disputes
the truths of Callaway and Moore and makes them out to be li-
ars. While Callaway's argument did rely solely on her opinion, she
was attempting to focus on the overwhelming perception problem
in Grand Saline. Moore's claims had more personal and firsthand
evidence. Nonetheless, the authors frame their article as the con-
crete "truth" on this subject and dismiss anyone who might disagree
with them because of their prominence in town, their "historical
research," and their blessing from local historian Allen. Moore's
act called for a serious discussion about racism in the community,
but the reaction from community leaders was to simply dismiss his
death. As in the first article in the *Sun*, they never name him and
only mention him and the self-immolation in passing.

Historian and sociologist James Loewen, who wrote the famous
book *Sundown Towns*, states that "the best way to stay all-white,
many communities concluded, . . . [was to have] a reputation for
vicious white supremacy circulated among African Americans for
many miles around" (275). His research dives into all the various
sociological (and sometimes even rhetorical) factors that create sundown communities and illuminates the rhetorical hoops that these
prominent town residents jump through in their letter. Loewen's
research finds that historians and historical societies in sundown
towns often suppress truth (206) and that towns rely upon silencing in order to exclude (201). Going a step further, his research dis-
covers that local newspapers typically remain quiet when it comes
to discussing these issues, but when they aren't silent, they typically
disappear (203). The *Grand Saline Sun* didn't disappear following the coverage of racism by Wendi Callaway; however, Callaway
herself was terminated soon after. The letter written by prominent
Grand Saline citizens exists as a means to rhetorically dissociate
Grand Saline from racism, which could be a good response if they
actually dealt with the perception of the town, all of the historical
facts, and oral histories of the town. However, they fail to look
at this history and try only to suggest that Callaway is a liar and
Moore was wrong.

All of these various silences and erasures of Moore's life and death
are connected to white supremacy. As I have mentioned throughout

this book, white supremacy is built around preservation, and these silences and erasures of Moore are acts that preserve Grand Saline's white supremacist culture. None of the silencing of Moore—from the way his story was first presented in the *Sun*, to the challenges to his actions and how they are related to history, to the way his memory has been physically erased—is a literal manifestation of white supremacy. But these acts all *maintain* white supremacy. They are collective defenses that keep Moore from the limelight because if he gains national attention, as he did with *Man on Fire*, then the town might have to confront their history. Or, in other terms, the town challenges the memory of Moore to keep their culture intact. If they effectively erase all mentions of Moore from the memory of the town—by not even naming him in the letter from town gatekeepers and by tearing down memorials in his honor—then they won't have to answer to questions of racism. The white supremacy of the community maintains blinders for people's ideologies and keeps them from questioning dissenters and the evidence.

SELF-SILENCING AND SUPPRESSION IN *MAN ON FIRE*

I witnessed silencing in the various stages of producing *Man on Fire*, especially in terms of *self-silencing* and stifling promotion of the film. I'll begin with self-silencing. As Janet Swim and her coauthors write, "The discrepancy between wanting to say something and not saying something can be described as self-silencing. . . . Although self-silencing may *appear* to be a choice, it is done within a social context that can impose negative consequences for speaking one's voice" (494, emphasis mine). Swim et al. not only describe the act of self-silencing but unfold the rhetorical climate in which self-silencing exists—when a person wants to speak but fears what a community might say or do in response to this speech act. Most of the scholarship surrounding self-silencing in interdisciplinary terms focuses on these acts in regard to gendered discourse, emphasizing how these acts affect women and trans people in academia (London et al.), women's health (Maji and Dixit), and rural women coping with aging (Bogar et al.). In her article on silencing, Cheryl Glenn states:

When silence is our rhetorical choice, we can use it purposefully and productively, but when it is not our choice, but someone else's for us, it can be insidious, particularly when someone else's choice for us comes in the shape of institutional structure. To wit, a person can choose silence, but the choice isn't really his or hers because speaking out will be professional suicide. In short, he or she's been disciplined—and silenced. ("Silence," pp. 263–64)

Silencing can be empowering, but self-silencing in response to institutional power, or systemic structures, is often "insidious." The same thought applies to self-silencing in Grand Saline.

Self-silencing is an important concept to name because the culture not only silences those who have spoken but challenges people not to speak in the first place. Before even beginning film production, my producing partner Joel Fendelman and I knew that this would be a difficult endeavor. In our scouting trip to Grand Saline during May 2016, we found there were plenty of residents who had something to say when it came to claiming that the town isn't racist, but people who might be more liberal in their racial ideologies might tell us their thoughts but wouldn't want to be filmed.

When it came to Sandy Packer's not wanting to speak to us, self-silencing was clearly on display. She mentioned in her conversation with me the repercussions of teenagers asking around about race and racism, illustrating that she knew the consequences of going public about these types of issues. In this sense, Grand Saline doesn't even have to say anything to her. The historical record of what happens when someone speaks about racism—including the teenage journalism students' silencing and Callaway's firing—conveys to people that they need to know about these consequences. These types of self-silencing acts are rhetorically more effective too. No one has to threaten or harm someone; instead they just rely on the historical record as evidence for what can take place.

As a tool for white supremacy, self-silencing becomes a built-in defense for racists. No one has to threaten anyone for people to be quiet and not speak out, and if challenged on the culture of silencing people can argue it is just fake and perceived. Truthfully, many people might be able to speak out as prominent residents of Grand Saline and not have bad outcomes other than a few stares and whispers in the background. That might be a possibility. However, it doesn't undermine the accounts of the school journalists and Callaway, which are proof of the more extreme consequences of speaking out. So why would many people want to risk helping their community when they know they could potentially lose their jobs or be ousted from the comfort of their homes? Though we all want people to do the right thing, that is a big ask.

Silencing during our film's production didn't just occur with the self-silencing of interviewees but also ensued during the publicity for the film. I interacted with people in Grand Saline and surrounding areas on two separate occasions during the promotion of the film: once before a public screening in Tyler, Texas, which we invited all participants and anyone interested in the film to attend, and once before our national television premiere on PBS. The public screening took place on February 28, 2018, and the television premiere occurred on December 17, 2018. On both occasions, we dealt with silencing in promoting Moore's story and racial issues in Grand Saline via discussions with editors of newspapers and in social media comments from these newspapers' Facebook pages. One of the first emails I sent went to an editor in a town near Grand Saline and talked about the film and what we were trying to accomplish with a public screening—a real, public conversation on racism. While many papers in the area, such as the *Tyler Morning Telegraph*, helped promote the film, the editor of one regional paper in her response to me dismissed Moore's motives, expressed the belief that I was a race-baiter, and said she thought the film might be a hit-piece on Grand Saline.

She *assumed* that I *assumed* the entire town is racist. It's not just that she didn't promote the film (which would have been fine). She, of course, has full control of what content goes into her weekly paper. Rather, she attempted to silence the discussion of Moore and racism in Grand Saline by insinuating that Moore had a mental illness and by insinuating that since the film talks about racism in Grand Saline we would be "painting an entire town of people with a broad brush." Her comment on mental illness implies that any discussion of Moore that suggested he wasn't mentally ill would be wrong. The only explanation for his death would be mental illness.

More important, though, her narrative of the "racist" Black man who does as much harm to a white woman as is done to "someone who experiences racism" is a dismissive logical fallacy too. Who knows whether the story she tells really happened, but if so, someone—in a single moment—being labeled racist because they live in Grand Saline is not the same as someone experiencing racism on a daily basis on individual and systemic levels. Nevertheless, her warning on essentializing the community of Grand Saline comes from a good place (I hope), and she is right that researchers and documentarians must consider how they frame people and communities in their work. But in this case, she applies this warning as a way to discredit attempts to talk about racism in Grand Saline at all, to silence me and the film as stereotyping a community without knowing exactly what we are doing. Ironically, she seems to be painting the documentary with a broad brush herself since she had not watched it.

Other emails to the *Grand Saline Sun*, one asking for publicity surrounding the free public screening in Tyler and the other concerning the TV premiere on PBS, accomplished nothing. The editor replied, "Thank you!" to one request about promoting the film but chose not to promote it on the *Grand Saline Sun* Facebook page or in the paper. A few newspapers in the area did promote the film on their social media pages. *Van Zandt News*, the county paper for Grand Saline, posted a promotion for the PBS screening on December 5, 2018, two weeks removed from the premiere. Most of the comments consisted of people tagging others to show them the film, but many of the comments attempted to stifle the work as well. "Why can't they just leave this be and let the poor man and his family have peace," wrote one user. Another commenter responded, "Because the person who created this garbage needs it to boost is [sic] his credentials in academic circles and will create whatever narrative they needs [sic] in order to do it." Someone else wrote, "Stir up more hate because of the past . . . no thanks." Another individual asked, "This serves what purpose?" Most of the comments that didn't tag people were—in essence—moves to suggest people shouldn't engage with the film.

None of the commenters nor the editor of the newspaper who responded had seen the documentary prior to making these comments. They assumed that the film team was making terrible assumptions about the town, and they based this upon comments about me, knowing me, or just guessing what the film would cover.[2]

In Grand Saline, arguments that suppress conversations about racism actually preserve white supremacy because white supremacy is already the underbelly of the community—it exists even if no one says it does, or legends of it persist even if they are unsubstantiated. Until a public discourse opens up and labels this problem and attempts to fix it, all attempts to hinder racial discussions effectively protect white supremacy because they allow this perception to persist. Without acknowledging the legacy of racism, people in the community remain in denial of their own perception and their own problems. Openly admitting they have a problem would provide them the chance to acknowledge other people's perspectives while granting them a space to move forward by working with people in their community and people of color in nearby communities.

Silencing is an effective tactic of white supremacy because it relies upon quieting critiques of communal racism. Be it through the silencing of Moore's narrative and death in newspaper editorials or by erasing the memory of where he burned, or be it the silencing in interviews for the film and or in promotion of it, there is ample evidence to see the rhetorical nature of silencing as a tool that keeps oppression intact in Grand Saline.

In a poignant interview, a local Dallas–Fort Worth theologian, Jeff Hood, declared passionately to me, "My issue with Grand Saline is that it is easier to move past [Charles Moore's death], rather than sitting with it." In some sense, he defined the problem with silencing. It is much easier to label Moore's death as the act of a "crazy" man or to suggest there are no racism issues in the community. Sweeping problems under the rug is effortless. Yet, while many want the dismissal of these discussions to be further evidence that there are no problems in the community, my analysis displays how silencing becomes a tool to protect their community and its bigotry.

However, Grand Saline's silencing could also be an exigency for Moore's self-immolation too. In a social climate where nothing changes because no one talks about the issues—or when they talk about the issues they get ridiculed or fired from their jobs—what would suffice? Moore's stepdaughter, Kathy Renfro, thought this is why Moore self-immolated: "I think he was in such a place to where he had given so many words that he felt like words were no longer enough." He had to approach racism in Grand Saline in a different way. Many people question the efficacy of Moore's act: Why not just write letters to the editor? Why not create a sign? Why not march down Main Street?

I get it. There are no easy answers here, and typical types of protest might not have garnered much attention either.

In the end, Renfro might be right—words may no longer have been enough, either for Charles Moore or for Grand Saline.

7

Salty

One night, while I was interviewing people at a local all-you-can-eat fish buffet near Grand Saline, a sixty-year-old white man I knew (a former parishioner of my grandfather's church) told me a story about a Black minister who was the interim pastor at Main Street Baptist Church in Grand Saline for about a year, from 2014 to 2015. I asked him why the minister left: "Because he was run out of town. That's what happens in Grand Saline," he claimed.

This story had the potential to be explosive if true, and since I had known this person for over a decade and had no reason to believe he would lie to me, I contacted the former interim minister, Richard Taylor, to see whether he would participate in *Man on Fire*. Taylor hesitated at first because I think he knew why I had contacted him. "I only have nice things to say about the town," he stated to me, with certainty, on the phone. This puzzled me, and I couldn't tell if he was lying to me (Why would he lie?) or if this was his honest opinion. Eventually, after my persuading him over a couple of phone calls, he agreed to meet us at his office at the Southern Baptist Convention office in the Dallas–Fort Worth metroplex.

Before agreeing to be filmed, Taylor's in-office legal team looked over the filming agreement contract, and during this time it became apparent that he more than likely was not run out of town. He wasn't going to tell us some fantastical story of racism that occurred in his life because he didn't see any racism to name. To this day, I am uncertain why my grandfather's friend told me that he was kicked out of town for being Black, something that should have been acknowledged in Taylor's interview. Was it just someone being mistaken or misinformed? Or was it a blatant lie? I'll probably never know. Nonetheless, I was still eager to interview Taylor, because, even though he said he wouldn't express any ill will toward Grand Saline, he could offer some interesting perspective as a Black man who traveled a hundred miles every Sunday for a year to preach in this community. (He had decided not to live in town because he was only an interim pastor.)

Most of his interview was anything but revealing. He claimed that he loved the church and his parishioners and that they had fondly received him as well. He told us that they had actually voted to have him as the full-time minister, but that he declined because he wanted to do more work for the Southern Baptist Convention. However, perhaps his most telling response came in a question about racism, after he declined to say that he found any systemic bigotry in the community. "I do have one example, though," he proclaimed, while smiling into the camera:

> One morning [at church] I had a gentleman who came to me with tears in his eyes. He said: "Ten years ago, I would have hated you. Not because you have said anything wrong to me, just merely because of the color of your skin. I was taught to hate people like you. And after ministering with you . . . I love you. I'm angry at my parents for what they taught me because what they taught me was wrong." With tears in his eyes, he said, "Will you forgive me?" And with love and an embrace, "Of course I forgive you."

Regardless of our opinions of religion or evangelical Christianity, I found this anecdote full of answers, answers about ways we might change white supremacist cultures over time. Richard Taylor's time in the town is testimony to this.

Still, this story also illuminates the storytelling tradition in Grand Saline. The simple, supposed truth that Taylor just wanted to work for the convention would be an easy story to convey to locals, yet somehow—some way—a narrative formed that he was run out of town. This narrative *couldn't* exist unless Grand Saline's racist reputation wasn't palpable for residents. The story wouldn't make sense without the historical context of their being a racist community. So even though the stories of Grand Saline's racism seem to be more about historical incidents than contemporary ones, contemporary narratives of racism within the community ensure that the town's reputation never dissipates.

My research has investigated acts of white supremacy—acts that aren't always perceived as explicit bigotry—and shone a light on their effects, their means of persuasion, and their fallacies. I discuss growing up in Grand Saline and living around a culture comfortable saying the "n-word" and the ways I was made white or Brown under different rhetorical circumstance to illustrate how these cultures foster racial identity and indoctrinate and assimilate people into white supremacy. I share the various storytelling practices in Grand Saline—stories of the KKK, lynchings, and sundown towns—to emphasize how storytelling becomes a generative form of white supremacy by consistently marking Black people as "other" and still making people of color fearful of the community. I pinpoint the practice of rhetorical silencing as a means for people in Grand Saline to shut down dissent and erase narratives of antiracism, leaving people ignorant of these issues within the community and leaving racial objectors discredited or unheard.

While Grand Saline might be peculiar in some of its rhetorical practices, it is not the only small town in the United States that is dominated by white supremacy. Typically, after public screenings of *Man on Fire*, one or two people come up to me and say something to the effect of, "Wow! Grand Saline sounds like my hometown" or, "This reminds me of a town near me." This isn't just a phenomenon in the South. As James Loewen indicates in his research on sundown towns (one type of white supremacist community), they exist all across the United States and are actually more prevalent in northern communities. Towns like Grand Saline exist in every single state. We are never too far removed from them, even if we don't live in these communities. This book analyzes Grand Saline so that we can better identify these types of towns, so they don't always hide behind platitudes like "We aren't *that* racist" or "It's not about race, it's about [fill in the blank]."

In this way, *Salt of the Earth* isn't only a rhetorical analysis or an autoethnographic study. It's also an appeal to morality. For too long, we have given white supremacy a pass in society. We want to be polite, or we don't want to offend, or we think maybe over time people will change, or we believe once the people with older mindsets die that things will be different. That is not the case. This book emphasizes the ways that white supremacy thrives in the twenty-first century, yes, but there's also another clear conclusion: White supremacy is built to survive and evolve. We see this through the history of white supremacy nationally and with Grand Saline, a town that has been plagued with white supremacy for at least a century and has faced zero consequences, besides some bad press every now and then.

White supremacy will thrive as long as we let it survive, and thus what we must do, as rhetoricians and members of the public at large, is confront it wherever possible. The answer to racism isn't silence; the answer is speaking out. That is the least we can do. We need to name these communities. We need to challenge them. We need to have public conversations with and in them. We need them to know that we see them and that we are fighting for them to change. That should be our first response. Ever since I started working on my dissertation on Grand Saline six years ago, the community's white supremacy has been more public (not just through me, but through the various articles written about Moore's self-immolation and the town). Any given week I get dozens of hits on my blog with people searching "Grand Saline" and "racism" or "sundown town." Though not everyone in the community has changed because of Moore's death or my work, they have started conversations. And that's our first step of action, to put white supremacy in the spotlight.

CHANGING GRAND SALINE
Salt preserves, as I write in the introduction of this book.

But salt also corrodes.

In Texas, it is customary for college students to go to South Pa-
dre Island (at the bottom of the state near the Mexican border)
during spring break every year. Every time we would take off for
this twelve-hour trek during March, my grandfather would repeat
the same advice to me: "Once you get home you need to wash your
car because the salt will corrode it from underneath!" People who
live near the beach routinely wash their cars because the salt from
the ocean can corrode its underbelly. Now that I live in New England, I hear similar stories stemming from salting the roads during
snowstorms: Wash your car—especially the underbelly—every few
weeks in the winter, to keep the salt off. As I have argued throughout this book, whiteness preserves, but that act of preservation also
damages. It's harmful. So what can we do to change it?

That's the number one question people ask me about Grand
Saline. How can they change? Sometimes this is an honest question
meant to highlight people's unwillingness to evolve. Other times,
this is a defensive act. If my work doesn't change anything, what is
the purpose? Below I detail some (im)practical steps Grand Saline
could take to change their perceptions and ideologies. These aren't
the only ways the town can progress, nor are they always easy. Still,
this is what we must do to battle communal bigotry.

Host public conversations. One of the first steps Grand Saline
could take would be to hold a public conversation about their racism and their history. This would give them the chance to have an
actual discussion with real people, instead of just defending themselves privately. It could be a public event where people from Grand
Saline and surrounding communities of color could get together
to talk. I think this would be positive, even if it weren't fruitful,
because it would show a willingness to change or an acceptance
that there is something wrong here. The public nature of the event
could humble us all. If a community comes forward and wants to
change, who will view them negatively?

Listen. On this end, Grand Saline could change—with a public event or without—by actually listening to people who note
problems. Various examples of rhetorical scholarship, including
Krista Ratcliffe's *Rhetorical Listening* and Wayne Booth's *Rhetoric*

of RHETORIC, emphasize the importance of being in a space with others and hearing them actually speak. Residents should emphasize listening as a practice, actually hearing the words and pain that others express about racism in the area, taking their words as individual truth, and not just assuming the person speaking to them is wrong or is lying. Such a framework is how I first started hearing about people believing that Grand Saline is racist, as one of my best friends in college, Michael McClendon, a Black man, grew up ten miles south of the town. Taking his words and fears as a reality opened my eyes to the issues many people have with my hometown. Listening is of the utmost importance to changing views.

Be vulnerable and not defensive. In a similar vein, when given opportunities to listen and speak about racism, people in the community shouldn't move right into defensive modes. None of us wants to be defined by our worst attributes or biases, and so a public conversation might lead people into wanting to defend themselves. But they shouldn't. It's okay to state your opinions and views and be heard. However, such conversations would be pointless if people just defended themselves and didn't listen. Vulnerability is key to change because then our weaknesses are made public, and we know that we can improve. I often attempt to embody this in my classroom space by correcting myself when misspeaking. Being honest and reflective with ourselves is paramount.

Demonstrate learning/change. Finally, conversations like this would be pointless if they just ended with the conversation itself. To fully commit to changing white supremacy, people need to demonstrate what they are learning, and how they are implementing changes into their town's culture, their local government, their schools, and more. Maybe the school should create a curriculum that combats the racist storytelling that every kid in town hears and repeats. Maybe the museums in the town could add sections that talk about their history and perceptions of their racism. This could illustrate a commitment to actual change, instead of just saying, "We will be better," while doing nothing. And—perhaps—this commitment is what it would truly take to overhaul white supremacy, a commitment that understands that everything will not be perfect overnight but that people are truthfully trying to better themselves, their home, and their relationships with their neighbors.

These are not all of the answers. I doubt anyone has those. But these are some fundamental steps that Grand Saline could take to actually change and alter the way they are perceived.

ON BEING SALTY

On Urban Dictionary.com, *salty* has been defined as "the act of being upset, angry, or bitter as a result of being made fun of or embarrassed. Also a characteristic of a person who feels out of place or is feeling attacked." I get salty when I lose in a video game (especially a sports video game) or when my friends gang up on me in the group chat. Everyone gets salty sometimes. Yet many in Grand Saline have attributed the past seven years of my work—from writing the dissertation, to making the film, to completing this book—to saltiness. Many have argued with me, publicly and privately, and claim that I have either exploited Grand Saline or am just mad about my high school life.

They believe I am salty.

The truth is, I loved my time in Grand Saline. I met some amazing people, had some wonderful friends, and enjoyed my high school experience. I don't deny any of this. However, I also acknowledge that my memories of my hometown are clouded by the racism I described in these chapters—a racism that defined me in high school as "Wetback" or "Beaner" to some and a racism that led to an exceptional act of solidarity to take place, Charles Moore's self-immolation. I can't deny these facts either.

With all of this said, I end this book with a promise—something I vowed to myself seven years ago now, something that many of you may attribute to my own saltiness.

Grand Saline is adamant that they don't want public reminders of Charles Moore, seen in the way people treated his death in the newspaper, the lack of discourse surrounding his self-immolation, the quick erasure of his narrative, and the dismissal of *Man on Fire*.

As someone who studies trauma and public memory, I can't help thinking that one of the best ways to help Grand Saline evolve is to provide them with a permanent reminder of what happened in town on June 23, 2014, the day Charles Moore lit himself on fire. The Texas State Historical Commission (TSHC) states that you cannot petition for a memorial in honor of someone who has died until ten years after their death (rules that seem a bit arbitrary). I believe Moore's life is historically significant and that he deserves such a plaque, not just to honor what he did, but in hopes that such a plaque might influence the community in the future.

So here is my promise to you, Grand Saline.

On June 23, 2024, on the ten-year anniversary of Moore's death, I will submit the required paperwork with the TSHC to claim that Charles Moore—and his death—are historically significant and will ask that a public memorial be constructed in his honor.

I won't do this out of anger or hatred or saltiness but out of love for the town I once called home, a town Moore cared about so much that he gave up his life as a protest to change racism in the community.

I can only hope that such a marker will help persuade the community to publicly deal with its racist culture.

NOTES

1. *Whoosh*

1. In this book, I use pseudonyms for many—but not all—people. Typically, I give pseudonyms to people who wish to be unidentified or people I name in my personal memories and stories. Most people who signed film waivers—thus giving their permission to be public—do not have pseudonyms.

2. In this book, I will never repeat words or phrases of explicit racism because I don't want to replicate the historical and contemporary harm done with such epithets. You can assume what took place in these moments, but that isn't important. Rather, I intend only to emphasize the harm done in such instances when racism occurred. It is more important that we focus on the mechanisms of white supremacy—such as the ways they (dis)invite Brown bodies into/ from those spaces—than on what was actually said.

3. The Pew Research Center indicates that most Latinx people claim that "language skills" are the "biggest cause of discrimination" for them ("Perceptions").

4. On March 2, 2017, the infamous pseudoscientist Charles Murray was scheduled to speak on Middlebury's campus. However, students chanted Murray off the stage, and when he left the school he was met with protestors blocking his path. The incident was met with immediate backlash ("Discord"; Bruni; Jaschik).

2. The In-Between

1. I use this term similarly to the way Wayne Booth refers to "motivism" in his book *Modern Dogma and the Rhetoric of Assent*. He refers to the way people tend to motivize when they disagree with someone—we are more likely to argue that someone is arguing out of bad faith, or that their motives are not pure, than to take them at their word.

2. It should be noted that many of Lincoln's responses consisted of his

saying, "Nothing racist really happened to me, but one time. . . ." and then he would mention an explicitly racist memory. He might have been cognitively dissociating from these incidents of racism, held a different definition of racism, or been made nervous by the camera.

3. The Truth about Stories

1. Confederate memorials were built to terrorize Black folks (Gardner) and were built by organizations who aligned themselves with explicit racism, like the United Daughters of the Confederacy (Palmer and Wessler).

4. Where There's Smoke

1. James Byrd Jr., a forty-nine-year-old Black man, was murdered by three white supremacists in Jasper, who dragged him from the back of their truck until he was decapitated. Two of the murderers were given the death penalty and one was sentenced to life imprisonment (Burch). Byrd's death became a national story, and his name was used for the Matthew Shepard and James Byrd Jr. Hate Crimes Prevention Act, signed by President Barack Obama in 2009, which expanded hate crimes to include those motivated by a victim's gender identity, sexual orientation, or disability.
2. Translated as "communities that come together for a mutual benefit."
3. Literally, "s/he is lying" but translated as "Cherokee storytelling."
4. See Gillian Brockell's "She Was Stereotyped as 'The Welfare Queen'" in the *Washington Post*.
5. I am not claiming statistical significance in this book.
6. This interview was recorded in the summer of 2016.
7. While I can appreciate Allen's perspective, I disagree with him. It would be a reasonable argument that the editor sensationalized this story to sell newspapers if it were the cover story of the paper, but the incident was on the bottom of Page 1, having no big headline that would attract an audience. If the goal was simply to fabricate a story to sell papers, then why bury it at the bottom of the first page?

5. "But Once Was Enough"

1. Joel and I often debate the ethics of this encounter. Is it okay not to tell the whole truth if it helps you get more information for your story? We actually created a "Documentary Ethics" workshop built

around this question that we have presented at a few universities around the country.

6. Silenced

1. The editorial has since been deleted from the page, but the town's response to her that was published in the *Sun* newspaper can be found in the July 17, 2014, edition of the paper. I discuss this later in the chapter.
2. It is worth noting that most Grand Saline residents who contacted me following the release of the film had only positive things to say and claimed some version of: "It wasn't as bad as I thought it would be!," which is telling in itself.

WORKS CITED

Adams, Sam. Personal interview. 2 July 2016.

Alaniz, Yolanda, and Megan Cornish. *Viva la Raza: A History of Chicano Identity and Resistance*. Red Letter Press, 2008.

Alcoff, Linda Martín. "Latino/as, Asian Americans, and the Black-White Binary." *The Journal of Ethics*, vol. 7, no. 1, Mar. 2003, pp. 5–27.

Allen, Elvis. Personal interview. 3 July 2016.

Anderson, Benedict. *Imagined Communities: Reflections on the Origin and Spread of Nationalism*. 1982. Verso, 2006.

Anderson, Carol. *White Rage*. Bloomsbury, 2016.

Applebaum, Barbara. "'Listening Silence' and Its Discursive Effects." *Educational Theory*, vol. 66, no. 3, 2016, pp. 389–404.

Bamberg, Michael. "Considering Counter Narratives." *Considering Counter-Narratives: Narrating, Resisting, Making Sense*, edited by Bamberg and Molly Andrews, John Benjamins Publishing, 2004, pp. 351–72.

Bednar, Robert M. "Killing Memory: Roadside Memorial Removals and the Necropolitics of Affect." *Cultural Politics*, vol. 9, no. 3, 2013, pp. 337–56.

———. "Materialising Memory: The Public Lives of Roadside Crash Shrines." *Memory Connection Journal*, vol. 1, no. 1, 2011, pp. 18–33.

Bell, Chuck. "Stone Mountain a Leader in Region Tourism." *The Atlanta Journal-Constitution*, 12 June 1986, rpt. 26 Apr. 2017, www.ajc.com/entertainment/attractions/stone-mountain-leader-region-tourism/QD8S2cqzAlUBjK7s2wq45N. Accessed 7 Apr. 2020.

Bell, Shelby P. "What Does Silence Signify? Investigating the Rhetoric of Silence in *Berghuis v. Thompkins*." *Western Journal of Communication*, vol. 78, no. 2, 2014, pp. 175–93.

Berman, Mark, and Ben Guarino. "Mississippi Governor Signs Bill Changing State's Flag, Abandoning Confederate Symbol." *The Washington Post*, 30 June 2020, www.washingtonpost.com/national/mississippi-flag-confederacy-removed/2020/06/30/f47df152-baed-11ea-8cf5-9c1b8d7f84c6_story.html. Accessed 17 Aug. 2020.

Bever, Lindsey. "A Texas Minister Set Himself on Fire and Died to 'Inspire' Justice." *The Washington Post*, 16 July 2014, www.washington post.com/news/morning-mix/wp/2014/07/16/79-year-old-retired-reverend-set-himself-on-fire-to-inspire-social-justice/. Accessed 16 July 2014.

Beverley, John. *Testimonio: On the Politics of Truth.* U of Minnesota P, 2004.

Beydoun, Khaled A. *American Islamophobia: Understanding the Roots and Rise of Fear.* U of California P, 2018.

Bobic, Igor. "He Would Never Say It, But This Is Donald Trump's Favorite Rhetorical Device." *HuffPost.com*, 16 Feb. 2016, www.huffpost .com/entry/donald-trump-rhetorical-device_n_56c358cbe4b0c3c550 52b32b. Accessed 15 Apr. 2020.

Bogar, Sandra, et al. "Raising Rural Women's Voices: From Self-Silencing to Self-Expression." *Journal of Women and Aging*, vol. 29, no. 6, 2017, pp. 515–29.

Bonilla-Silva, Eduardo. *Racism without Racists: Color-Blind Racism and Racial Inequality in Contemporary America.* 3rd ed., Rowman & Littlefield, 2009.

Booth, Wayne C. *Modern Dogma and the Rhetoric of Assent.* U of Chicago P, 1974.

———. *The Rhetoric of RHETORIC: The Quest for Effective Communication.* Blackwell Publishing, 2004.

Boylorn, Robin M., and Mark P. Orbe. *Critical Autoethnography: Intersecting Cultural Identities in Everyday Life.* Routledge, 2016.

Brayboy, Bryan McKinley Jones. "Hiding in the Ivy: American Indian Students and Visibility in Elite Educational Settings." *Harvard Educational Review*, vol. 74, no. 2, Summer 2004, pp. 125–52.

Brockell, Gillian. "She Was Stereotyped as 'The Welfare Queen': The Truth Was More Disturbing, a New Book Says." *The Washington Post.* 21 May 2019. www.washingtonpost.com/history/2019/05/21/she-was-ste reotyped-welfare-queen-truth-was-more-disturbing-new-book-says/. Accessed 7 Mar. 2020.

Bruni, Frank. "The Dangerous Safety of College." *The New York Times*, 11 Mar. 2017, www.nytimes.com/2017/03/11/opinion/sunday/the-dangerous-safety-of-college.html. Accessed 7 Mar. 2020.

Burch, Audra D. S. "In Texas, a Decades-Old Hate Crime, Forgiven but Never Forgotten." *The New York Times,* 9 July 2018, www.nytimes .com/2018/07/09/us/james-byrd-jasper-texas-killing.html. Accessed 5 Mar. 2020.

Callaway, Wendi. "Man Sets Himself on Fire in Public Parking Lot." *Grand Saline Sun*, 25 June 2014, p. 1.

———. "Protesting Racism." *Grand Saline Sun Facebook* page, 3 July 2014.

———. "Public Suicide about More than Just Racism." *Grand Saline Sun, TownNews.com*, 6 July 2014.

Campbell, Nikki Gaskins. "KKK Flyers Found in Goose Creek Subdivision." *The Berkeley Observer*, 2 May 2016, www.berkeleyobserver.com/2016/05/02/kkk-flyers-found-goose-creek-subdivision/. Accessed 22 June 2020.

Castagno, Angelina E. "Extending the Bounds of Race and Racism: Indigenous Women and the Persistence of the Black-White Paradigm of Race." *Urban Review*, vol. 37, no. 5, 2005, pp. 447–68.

Chang, Robert S. "Toward an Asian American Legal Scholarship: Critical Race Theory, Post-Structuralism, and Narrative Space." *California Law Review*, vol. 81, no. 5, 1993, pp. 1241–1323.

Chávez, Ernesto. "Chicano/a History: Its Origins, Purpose, and Future." *Pacific Historical Review*, vol. 82, no. 4, 2013, pp. 505–19.

Cicero, Marcus Tullius, and Stephen Ciraolo. *Cicero's Pro Caelio*. Bolchazy-Carducci Publishers, 1997.

Clark, Gregory. *Rhetorical Landscapes in America: Variations on a Theme from Kenneth Burke*. U of South Carolina P, 2004.

Colston, Chase. "Ku Klux Klan Members Distribute Flyers in East Texas Towns." *KNUE 101.5*, 16 Oct. 2014, knue.com/ku-klux-klan-members-distribute-flyers-in-east-texas-towns/. Accessed 12 June 2019.

Condon, Frankie. *I Hope I Join the Band: Narrative, Affiliation, and Antiracist Rhetoric*. Utah State UP, 2012.

Cook, Lisa D. "Converging to a National Lynching Database: Recent Developments and the Way Forward." *Historical Methods*, vol. 45, no. 2, 2012, pp. 55–63.

Crawford, Shirley. Personal interview. 19 June 2015.

Darity, William A., Jr., et al. "Bleach in the Rainbow: Latin Ethnicity and Preference for Whiteness." *Transforming Anthropology*, vol. 13, no. 2, 2005, pp. 103–09.

Dean, Kenneth. "Madman or Martyr? Retired Minister Sets Self on Fire, Dies." *Tyler Morning Telegraph*, 1 July 2014, pp. A1+.

Delgado, Richard. "Storytelling for Oppositionists and Others: A Plea for Narrative." *Michigan Law Review*, vol. 87, no. 8, 1989, pp. 2411–41.

Delgado, Richard, and Jean Stefancic. *Critical Race Theory: An Introduction*. 3rd ed., New York UP, 2017.

"Discord at Middlebury: Students on the Anti-Murray Protests." *The New York Times*. 7 Mar. 2017. www.nytimes.com/2017/03/07/opinion/discord-at-middlebury-students-on-the-anti-murray-protests.html. Accessed 7 Mar. 2020.

Eckert, Richard Clark. "Wennebojo Meets a 'Real Indian.'" *American Indian Rhetorics of Survivance: Word Medicine, Word Magic*. Ed. Ernest Stromberg. U of Pittsburgh P, 2006. 256–71.

Erwin, Emily. Personal interview. 14 July 2016.

Fahrenthold, David A. "Trump Recorded Having Extremely Lewd Conversation about Women in 2005." *Washington Post*, 7 Oct. 2016, www.washingtonpost.com/politics/trump-recorded-having-extremely-lewd-conversation-about-women-in-2005/2016/10/07/3b9ce776-8cb4-11e6-bf8a-3d26847eeed4_story.html. Accessed 28 June 2019.

Fite, B. R. Personal interview. 4 June 2016.

Frank, Reanne, et al. "Latino Immigrants and the U.S. Racial Order: How and Where Do They Fit In?" *American Sociological Review*, vol. 75, no. 3, 2010, pp. 378–401.

Garcia, Jose. Personal interview. 14 Aug. 2016.

Gardner, Sarah E. "What We Talk about When We Talk about Confederate Monuments." *Origins*, vol. 11, no. 5, 2018. origins.osu.edu/article/what-we-talk-about-when-we-talk-about-confederate-monuments. Accessed 22 Apr. 2020.

Gilyard, Keith. *Voices of the Self: A Study of Language Competence*. Wayne State UP, 1991.

Glenn, Cheryl. "Silence: A Rhetorical Art for Resisting Discipline(s)." *JAC*, vol. 22, no. 2, 2002, pp. 261–91.

———. *Unspoken: A Rhetoric of Silence*. Southern Illinois UP, 2004.

Goehring, Charles, and George N. Dionisopoulos. "Identification by Antithesis: *The Turner Diaries* as Constitutive Rhetoric." *Southern Communication Journal*, vol. 78, no. 5, 2013, pp. 369–86.

Guerra, Juan C. *Language, Culture, Identity, and Citizenship in College Classrooms and Communities*. Routledge and NCTE, 2016.

Gutiérrez-Jones, Carl. *Rethinking the Borderlands: Between Chicano Culture and Legal Discourse*. U of California P, 1995.

Halberstam, David. *The Making of a Quagmire: America and Vietnam during the Kennedy Era*. 1964. Rev. ed., edited by Daniel J. Singal, Rowman & Littlefield Publishing, 2008.

Hall, Michael. "Man on Fire." *Texas Monthly*, Dec. 2014, www.texasmonthly.com/articles/man-on-fire/. Accessed 15 Dec. 2014.

———. Personal interview. 16 May 2015.

Harper, Faith. "Morton's Salt Mine Continues to Produce." *Tyler Morning Telegraph*, 25 May 2013, tylerpaper.com/news/local/morton-s-salt-mine-continues-to-produce/article_a6d6c682-0fe8-541f-83b6-71cb31e1e39d.html. Accessed 27 May 2019.

Harris, Keshia L. "Biracial American Colorism: Passing for White." *American Behavioral Scientist*, vol. 62, no. 14, 2018, pp. 2072–86.

Hartman, Chester, and Gregory D. Squires, eds. *The Integration Debate: Competing Futures for American Cities*. Routledge, 2009.

Hawk, Byron. "A Rhetoric/Pedagogy of Silences: Sub-version in Paul Kameen's Writing/Teaching." *Pedagogy*, vol. 3, no. 3, 2003, pp. 377–97.

Heuman, Amy, and Catherine Langford. "Tradition and Southern Confederate Culture: Manifesting Whiteness through Public Memory at Texas A&M University." *Public Memory, Race, and Ethnicity*, edited by G. Mitchell Reyes, Cambridge Scholars Publishing, 2010, pp. 120–45.

Hing, Bill Ong. "Beyond the Rhetoric of Assimilation and Cultural Pluralism: Addressing the Tension of Separatism and Conflict in an Immigration-Driven Multiracial Society." *California Law Review*, vol. 81, no. 4, 1993, pp. 863–925.

Hood, Jeff. *The Passion of Charles Moore*. Resource Publications, 2019.

———. Personal interview. 15 Aug. 2016.

"I'm a Football Hero." *True Life*, produced by Lauren Lazin, season 2, episode 8, MTV, 21 Jan. 2000.

Jaschik, Scott. "The Aftermath at Middlebury." *Inside Higher Ed.* 6 Mar. 2017. www.insidehighered.com/news/2017/03/06/middlebury-engages-soul-searching-after-speech-shouted-down-and-professor-attacked. Accessed 7 Mar. 2020.

Jones, Amanda. Personal interview. 19 Aug. 2015.

"Jordan's Saline Massacre." *Grand Saline Sun*, 1909, Van Zandt County Historical Society Archives.

Kallen, Horace Meyer. *Culture and Democracy in the United States*. Boni and Liveright, 1924.

Keenan, Kate, and Joshua Keenan. Personal interview. 7 Aug. 2016.

King, Lisa, et al. "Introduction: Careful with the Stories We Tell: Naming Survivance, Sovereignty, and Story." *Survivance, Sovereignty, and Story: Teaching American Indian Rhetorics*, edited by King, Gubele, and Anderson, UP of Colorado, 2015, pp. 3–16.

King, Thomas. *The Truth about Stories: A Native Narrative*. U of Minnesota P, 2008.

Kleiner, Diana J. "Grand Saline, TX." *Handbook of Texas Online, Texas State Historical Association.com*, www.tshaonline.org/handbook/entries/grand-saline-tx. Accessed 12 Mar. 2021.

Knope, Billy. Personal interview. 17 Aug. 2016.

Lambert, Buddy. Personal interview. 13 June 2016.

Lea, James B., et al. "Letter to the Editor: Racism in Grand Saline? The Historical Truths." *Grand Saline Sun*, 14 July 2014, pp. 4+.

Legg, Emily. *Listening to Our Stories in Dusty Boxes: Indigenous Storytelling Methodology, Archival Practice, and the Cherokee Female Seminary.* 2016. Purdue University, PhD dissertation.

Lewis, Danny. "This Map Shows over a Century of Documented Lynchings in the United States." *Smithsonian.com*, 24 Jan. 2017, www.smithsonianmag.com/smart-news/map-shows-over-a-century-of-documented-lynchings-in-united-states-180961877/. Accessed 17 May 2019.

Lockett, Alexandria, et al. *Race, Rhetoric, and Research Methods.* WAC Clearinghouse, forthcoming.

Loewen, James W. *Sundown Towns: A Hidden Dimension of American Racism.* New Press, 2005.

———. *Sundown Towns in the United States*, sundown.tougaloo.edu/content.php?file=sundowntowns-whitemap.html.

London, Bonita, et al. "Gender-Based Rejection Sensitivity and Academic Self-Silencing in Women." *Journal of Personality and Social Psychology*, vol. 102, no. 5, 2012, pp. 961–79.

Lunsford, Tracy. Personal interview. 18 July 2015.

Maji, Sucharita, and Shikha Dixit. "Self-Silencing and Women's Health: A Review." *International Journal of Social Psychiatry*, vol. 65, no. 1, 2019, pp. 3–13.

Mann, Sasha. Personal interview. 9 June 2016.

Martinez, Aja Y. "Alejandra Writes a Book : A Critical Race Counterstory about Writing, Identity, and Being Chicanx in the Academy." *Praxis*, vol. 14, no. 1, 2016, pp. 56–61.

———. "'The American Way': Resisting the Empire of Force and Color-Blind Racism." *College English*, vol. 71, no. 6, 2009, 584–95.

———. *Counterstory: The Rhetoric and Writing of Critical Race Theory.* CCCC and NCTE, 2020.

———. "Critical Race Theory: Its Origins, History, and Importance to the Discourses and Rhetorics of Race." *Frame*, vol. 27, no. 2, 2014, pp. 9–27.

———. "A Plea for Critical Race Theory Counterstory: Stock Story versus Counterstory Dialogues Concerning Alejandra's 'Fit' in the Academy." *Composition Studies*, vol. 42, no. 2, 2014, pp. 33–55.

McClendon, Michael. Personal interview. 9 June 2016.

McCoy, Cory. "Filmmakers Hope Movie Fosters Conversation about Racial Divide." *Tyler Morning Telegraph*, 1 Mar. 2018, tylerpaper.com/filmmakers-hope-movie-fosters-conversation-about-racial-divide/article_1b77c8b4-fc2f-5062-9f1c-fc3c88d99912.html. Accessed 1 Mar. 2018.

Medina, Cruz. "Digital Latin@ Storytelling: *testimonio* as Multimodal Resistance." *Racial Shorthand: Coded Discrimination Contested in Social Media*. Edited by Medina and Octavio Pimentel. Computers and Composition Digital Press, 2018.

Michaels, Lacey. Personal interview. 29 July 2015.

Moore, Charles. "Last Appeal." 21 June 2014. Reverend Charles Moore Papers, 1945–2015. Dolph Briscoe Center for American History, U of Texas at Austin.

———. "Lazarus, Come Out!" 10 Oct. 1998. Reverend Charles Moore Papers, as above.

———. "O Grand Saline Repent of Your Racism." 23 June 2014. Reverend Charles Moore Papers, as above.

———. "You Give Them Something to Eat." Reverend Charles Moore Papers, as above.

Moore, Guy. Personal interview. 26 July 2016.

Morgan, Scott. "For Many Black Texans, Grand Saline Embodies Racism. So Is That Fair?" *KETR.org*. 17 Dec. 2018. www.ketr.org/post/many-black-texans-grand-saline-embodies-racism-so-fair. Accessed 18 Dec. 2018.

Morris, Charles E., III. "Pink Herring and the Fourth Persona : J. Edgar Hoover's Sex Crime Panic." *Quarterly Journal of Speech*, vol. 88, no. 2, 2002, pp. 228–44.

Morrison, Lisa. Personal interview. 3 Aug. 2016.

Munn, Mallie. Personal interview. 8 July 2016.

Nunez-Smith, Marcella, et al. "Healthcare Workplace Conversations on Race and the Perspectives of Physicians of African Descent." *Journal of General Internal Medicine*, vol. 23, no. 9, 2008: 1471–76.

Olson, Christa J. *Constitutive Visons: Indigeneity and Commonplaces of National Identity in Republican Ecuador*. Pennsylvania State UP, 2014.

Omi, Michael, and Howard Winant. *Racial Formation in the United States*. 3rd ed., Routledge, 2014.

Packer, Sandy. Personal interview. 7 May 2015.

Palmer, Brian, and Seth Freed Wessler. "The Costs of the Confederacy." *Smithsonian Magazine*, Dec. 2018. www.smithsonianmag.com/history/costs-confederacy-special-report-180970731/. Accessed 22 Apr. 2020.

"Perceptions of Discrimination." Sec. 6 of the *2007 National Survey of Latinos*. Pew Research Center, www.pewhispanic.org/2007/12/13/iv-perceptions-of-discrimination/. Accessed 12 Apr. 2019.

Perea, Juan F. "The Black/White Binary Paradigm of Race: The 'Normal Science' of American Racial Thought." *California Law Review*, vol. 85, no. 5, 1997, pp. 1213–58.

Portes, Alejandro, and Rubén G. Rumbaut. *Immigrant America: A Portrait.* 4th ed., U of California P, 2014.

Powell, Malea, et al. "Our Story Begins Here: Constellating Cultural Rhetorics." *Enculturation,* 25 Oct. 2014. enculturation.net/our-story-begins-here. Accessed 3 May 2019.

Prasad, Vasundhara. "If Anyone Is Listening, #MeToo: Breaking the Culture of Silence around Sexual Abuse through Regulating Non-Disclosure Agreements and Secret Settlements." *Boston College Law Review*, vol. 59, no. 7, 2018.

Ratcliffe, Krista. *Rhetorical Listening: Identification, Gender, Whiteness.* Southern Illinois UP, 2005.

Renfro, Kathy. Personal interview. 18 Sept. 2016.

Repko, Melissa. "In Dying Act, Minister Hoped to Inspire Social Justice." *The Dallas Morning News*, 11 July 2014, www.dallasnews.com/news/2014/07/12/in-dying-act-minister-hoped-to-inspire-social-justice/. Accessed 12 Mar. 2021.

Rodriguez, Roberto. "The Origins and History of the Chicano Movement." Occasional Paper No. 7, Julian Samora Research Institute, Michigan State U, Apr. 1996, pp. 1–6.

Ryan, Cynthia, "Unquiet Gestures: Thoughts on a Productive Rhetoric(s) of Silence." *JAC*, vol. 22, no. 3, 2002, 667–78.

"Salty." *Urban Dictionary*. 1 Feb. 2011. www.urbandictionary.com/define .php?term=salty. Accessed 7 June 2020.

Sanchez, James Chase, producer. *Man on Fire*. Directed by Joel Fendelman. New Day Films. 2018.

———. "Recirculating Our Racism: Public Memory and Folklore in East Texas." *Inventing Place: Writing Lone Star Rhetorics*. Edited by Casey Boyle and Jenny Rice. Southern Illinois UP, 2018, pp. 75–87.

———. "Trump, the KKK, and the Versatility of White Supremacy Rhetoric." *Journal of Contemporary Rhetoric*, vol. 8, no. 1/2, 2018, pp. 44–56.

Sium, Aman, and Eric Ritskes. "Speaking Truth to Power: Indigenous Storytelling as an Act of Living Resistance." *Decolonization: Indigeneity, Education, and Society*, vol. 2, no.1, 2013, pp. i–x.

Sloan, Wayne. Personal interview. 3 July 2016.

Smilges, J. Logan. "White Squares to Black Boxes: Grindr, Queerness, Rhetorical Silence." *Rhetoric Review*, vol. 38, no. 1, 2019, 79–92.

Solórzano, Daniel G., and Tara J. Yosso. "Critical Race Methodology: Counter-Storytelling as an Analytical Framework for Education Research." *Qualitative Inquiry*, vol. 8, no. 1, 2002, pp. 23–44.

Song, Miri. "Introduction: Who's at the Bottom? Examining the Claims about Racial Hierarchy." *Ethnic and Racial Studies*, vol. 27, no. 6, 2004, pp. 859–77.

Stanley, Christine A. "When Counter Narratives Meet Master Narratives in the Journal Editorial-Review Process." *Educational Researcher*, vol. 36, no. 1, 2007, pp. 14–24.

"Stepson-in-Law of Man Who Set Self on Fire in Grand Saline: Final Act Was 'Ultimate Sacrifice.'" *Tyler Morning Telegraph* 2 July 2014, tylerpaper.com/news/local/stepson-in-law-of-man-who-set-self-on-fire-in-grand-saline-final-act/article_4bc67b0b-da45-55ba-a5d4-59bcd61d360f.html. Accessed 2 July 2014.

Stewart, Richard. "Desegregation—'Nothing's . . . to Change in Grand Saline.'" *Houston Chronicle*, 17 Oct. 1993.

Stromberg, Ernest. "Rhetoric and American Indians: An Introduction." *American Indian Rhetorics of Survivance: Word Medicine, Word Magic*, edited by Stromberg, U of Pittsburgh P, 2006, pp. 5–12.

Swim, Janet, et al. "Self-Silencing to Sexism." *Journal of Social Issues*, vol. 66, no. 3, 2010, pp. 493–507.

Sylvester, Leon. Personal interview. 15 May 2015.

Taylor, Richard. Personal interview. 8 Oct. 2016.

"36 Texas Counties Prepare to Follow Vidor's Integration Efforts." *Galveston Daily News*, 8 Aug. 1994, p. 7A.

Tovar, Terry. Personal interview. 8 Aug. 2016.

Towns, Armond R. "That Camera Won't Save You! The Spectacular Consumption of Police Violence." *Present Tense*, vol. 5, no. 2, 2015, www.presenttensejournal.org/volume-5/that-camera-wont-save-you-the-spectacular-consumption-of-police-violence/.

Troncoso, Sergio. *Crossing Borders: Personal Essays*. Arte Público Press, 2011.

United States Census Bureau. "About [Race]." *Census.gov*, www.census.gov/topics/population/race/about.html. Accessed 10 Mar. 2020.

Veach, Becky. Personal interview. 14 May 2015.

Vickery, Don. Personal interview. 9 Sept. 2016.

Villanueva, Victor. *Bootstraps: From an American Academic of Color*. NCTE, 1993.

————. "On the Rhetoric and Precedents of Racism." *College Composition and Communication*, vol. 50, no. 4, 1999, pp. 645–61.

Villarosa, Linda. "Myths about Physical Racial Differences Were Used to Justify Slavery—and Are Still Believed by Doctors Today." *New York Times*, 14 Aug. 2019. www.nytimes.com/interactive/2019/08/14/magazine/racial-differences-doctors.html.

Villarreal, Daniel. "Why a 79-Year-Old Progressive Methodist Minister Burned Himself Alive." *Hornet*, 1 Dec. 2015, hornet.com/stories/charles-moore-suicide-self-immolation/. Accessed 5 Dec. 2015.

Walter, Bronwen. "Challenging the Black/White Binary: The Need for an Irish Category in the 2001 Census." *Patterns of Prejudice*, vol. 32, no. 2, 1998, pp. 73–86.

Ward, Pamela. "Austin Minister Ends Hunger Strike after Bishops Issue Statement on Gays." *Austin-American Statesman*, 6 May 1995.

————. "Methodist Minister Protests Gay Policy with Hunger Strike." *Austin-American Statesman*, 3 May 1995.

White, Rex. Personal interview. 16 Sept. 2016.

Wilkinson, Bettina Cuttaia. "Perceptions of Commonality and Latino-Black, Latino-White Relations in a Multiethnic United States." *Political Research Quarterly*, 67, no. 4, 2014, pp. 905–16.

Williams, Gregory Howard. *Life on the Color Line: The True Story of a White Boy Who Discovered He Was Black*. Plume, 1996.

Wilson, Jason. "FBI Now Classifies Far-Right Proud Boys as 'Extremist Group,' Documents Say." *The Guardian*, 19 Nov. 2018, www.theguardian.com/world/2018/nov/19/proud-boys-fbi-classification-extremist-group-white-nationalism-report. Accessed 20 June 2020.

Wilt, Diana. Personal interview. 5 July 2016.

Winters, Lucy. Personal interview. 19 Aug. 2015.

Woods, James. Personal interview. 23 June 2016.

Woodson, Ashley N. "'There Ain't No White People Here': Master Narratives of the Civil Rights Movement in the Stories of Urban Youth." *Urban Education*, vol. 52, no. 3, 2017, pp. 316–42.

Yant, Chet. Personal interview. 6 June 2016.

Young, Crawford. *The Politics of Cultural Pluralism*. U of Wisconsin P, 1976.

Young v. Pierce, United States District Court for the Eastern District of Texas, 628 F. Supp. 1037, 31 July 1985.

Zagacki, Kenneth S. "Constitutive Rhetoric Reconsidered: Constitutive Paradoxes in G. W. Bush's Iraq War Speeches." *Western Journal of Communication*, vol. 71, no. 4, 2007, pp. 272–93.

INDEX

AUTHOR

James Chase Sanchez is an assistant professor of writing and rhetoric at Middlebury College in Vermont. His research interests are in cultural and racial rhetorics, public memory, and protest, and his research has appeared in *College Composition and Communication, Pedagogy, Journal of Contemporary Rhetoric,* and *Present Tense.* He is also the coauthor of a book titled *Race, Rhetoric, and Research Methods.* Outside of his academic research, Sanchez produces documentaries that focus on issues of racism, trauma, and memory. His first feature documentary, *Man on Fire,* won an International Documentary Association Award in 2017 and aired on PBS via *Independent Lens* in 2018. He is currently finishing production of a second documentary, tentatively titled *In Loco Parentis,* which focuses on two elite New England boarding schools with a shared history of covering up sexual assault allegations.

BOOKS IN THE CCCC STUDIES IN WRITING & RHETORIC SERIES